Truth, Justice, & The American Way
The Life And Times Of Noel Neill
The Original Lois Lane

An Authorized Biography

By
Larry Thomas Ward

Nicholas Lawrence Books

Los Angeles ★ Colorado Springs ★ Baltimore

Library of Congress Control Number: 2003102859

© Copyright 2003 By Larry Thomas Ward

All Rights Reserved.

This work may not be reproduced or transmitted in any form or by any means, electronic or mechanical, including recording, photocopying, or by any storage and retrieval system, without the written permission of the publisher. Exceptions would include brief excerpts in connection with reviews or sales promotions. For information, contact the publisher at: Nicholas Lawrence Books, 932 Clover Avenue, Canon City, CO 81212.

Superman is a trademark of DC Comics, Inc. Use of the character name should not be construed as a challenge to any trademark status.

All photographs and illustrations reproduced in this book came from the personal collection of Noel Neill.

ISBN 0-9729466-0-8

Printed in the United States of America

First Edition

Truth, Justice, & The American Way
The Life And Times Of Noel Neill
The Original Lois Lane

An Authorized Biography

~ Dedication ~

To Noel

Hollywood, 1939

Truth, Justice, & The American Way
The Life And Times Of Noel Neill
The Original Lois Lane

~ *Table of Contents* ~

Introduction By Jack Larson 7

Chapter 1: The Early Years 9

Chapter 2: Noel Neill, Songbird! 23

Chapter 3: You Ought To Be In Pictures! 33

Chapter 4: Up, Up, & Away! Superman – The Serials 59

Chapter 5: Truth, Justice, & The American Way:
    The Adventures of Superman – The Television Years 71

Chapter 6: How Long Has It Been Since You've Sung – Sober? The 1957 Fair Tour 97

Chapter 7: Gee, Superman, Are We Ever Glad To See You! The College Shows 107

Chapter 8: Noel Neill Today 117

Epilogue By Noel 127

Recommended Reading 129

Appendix I 131
    Dance School Credits From Age 4 Years To Age 17 Years.

Appendix II 135
    Professional Performance Credits From Age 10 Years To Age 17 Years.

Appendix III 141
    Singing Performances After 1937.

Appendix IV 143
    Films From 1941 To 2002.

Appendix V 145
    Radio and Television Appearances From 1943 To 2002.

Appendix VI 149
    The 1957 Fair Tour With George Reeves

Appendix VII 151
    College Lectures From 1974 To 1978

Acknowledgements 155

Truth, Justice, & The American Way
The Life And Times Of Noel Neill
The Original Lois Lane

~ *Introduction* ~

I met Noel Neill for the first time in 1950 inside the automobile of our mutual agent, Jack Pomeroy. I recognized her from the "Henry Aldrich" movies but had never seen the Columbia serials of Superman, so I didn't know her as Lois Lane. And, of course, I hadn't become her second Jimmy Olsen by then, either. Acting jobs had been scarce in Hollywood due to the breakup of the movie theater chains and the popularity of live television from the East Coast. Several studios had closed down. Noel and I, like so many other players, had been dropped from our studios contract lists. There was no filmed TV then, so our hardworking agent would take us every so often around the remaining casting offices to say hello and to stir up some work for us. Trying to sell yourself for a movie role is not an ego-enhancing situation. I could feel that Noel was uncomfortable about it, and certainly I was. But that is, and was, show business.

Three years later we were working together as Lois and Jimmy on the popular Superman TV series filmed in "Hollywood, U.S.A." The studios had jumped on the television bandwagon and we were there for the ride. We were a hardworking crew of TV pioneers who enjoyed each other: George Reeves (Superman); Noel (Lois Lane); John Hamilton (Perry White); Bob Shayne (Inspector Henderson); and me as Jimmy Olsen. We all had been through the Hollywood movie mill and had the bruises to show for it. Our production, shooting on a tight budget, was not heavy on the usual movie amenities. Beautiful Noel, with one of the greatest figures in town, had to wear a secondhand wardrobe; and without a hairdresser, had to "do" her own hair at 6:00 o'clock each working morning. She was always a trouper, trying to stay perky, on time, well-rehearsed, and delivering her happy "Lois" for the camera. But she was sensitive to careless treatment and we all concerned ourselves in keeping each others spirits up. When a staff writer complemented me on one performance, he was told by an executive, "Don't flatter the kid, he's liable to ask for more money."

However, though all of us got "typed" by our popular characters and couldn't get other work, it was a wonderful experience and we would have gone on filming it happily through 1959, if our Superman hadn't ended in tragedy with George's death.

Noel and I have stayed friends through the ensuing years, through tribulations and tributes. As the show has never gone off the air, we remain forever young there to generations of Superman fans, but in our real lives, and in the decades of interviews, Noel has remained the brave, good and lovely but maturing friend that Jimmy Olsen and I always needed. She is the adorable person depicted in this biography.

Jack Larson
February 2003

Chapter 1:
The Early Years

THE EARLY YEARS

Winter came early to Minneapolis on Thanksgiving Day in 1920, as a thin blanket of snow covered the city. For David and LaVere Neill, this day meant giving thanks not only for a year of prosperity, but for the birth of their newborn baby daughter, Noel Darleen Neill.

Barely two years before, in 1918, David Neill was a working journalist in New York City covering the events in America's busiest and most prosperous city. He had just met LaVere Binger, recently widowed wife of Eugene Binger, a soldier in the United States Army who was killed on a battlefield in France. LaVere had traveled to New York from California to be closer to Eugene when she received the devastating news of her beloved's fate. Before he shipped off to the war in Europe, they had a child together, Eugene Binger, Jr. Upon hearing the news of the death of her husband, grief-stricken, LaVere made the difficult decision to send her young baby to California to live with his paternal grandparents, while she attempted to start a new life in New York.

Although less than five feet tall, LaVere always fancied herself to be a pretty good singer and dancer.

LaVere and Eugene Binger, Jr., 1917

She soon found steady work on many of the stages of New York's vaudeville theatres. It was on one such occasion that she met David Neill, a recent graduate of Wisconsin's Beloit College. David was a young and very ambitious journalism major who wanted nothing more than to report the news of the day. He had landed a very good position with Fairchild Publications, publisher of the national trade magazines, *Home Furnishings* and *Women's Wear Daily*. In only a few months he had made a good enough impression that he was sent to Minneapolis to cover Midwest fashion news for the latter publication. By the time he left New York, he had asked LaVere to be his bride. They were married in 1919 and began their lives together in south Minneapolis, eventually sharing the same home for more than forty years.

Although neither wealthy nor poor, David and LaVere found Minneapolis to be a good place to raise a family, and one year later, Noel was born. By all accounts, David and LaVere were very happy. With doting parents, Noel wanted for very little. Surviving photographs of this period show the beaming father proudly posing with his young daughter, or LaVere gracefully walking her toddler through a local

THE EARLY YEARS

Noel at ten months

park. They took turns pushing the baby carriage that held their precious gift, and their love for this child never seemed to waver, never waned. Although they were not prone to outward displays of affection, Noel never doubted how her parents truly felt about her.

Noel Neill's early childhood was unexceptional – a normal life for a normal Minneapolis child – except for another decision by LaVere that set into motion a course of action that would ultimately determine the direction of Noel's life.

As a former singer and dancer, LaVere always believed that her professional career was over long before it ever began. Marriage and motherhood gave her the security she needed, and personal satisfaction that she craved. Still, entertainment was in her blood and she desperately wanted to perform, but as the wife of a prominent citizen always in the public eye, such thoughts were considered improper during these provincial times. She loved show business, and early on saw that Noel seemed to also have the skill for the live stage. As early as three years of age, Noel was singing the tunes of the day, and she showed a talent for improvised dancing.

In 1925, at the age of four years, Noel was enrolled in Minneapolis' premier school for aspiring young actors and actresses, The Seton Guild of Dance and Dramatic Arts. Thus began a ten-year enrollment in no fewer than six separate schools catering to the young and talented.

The Seton Guild was run by Genevieve Ward, the director of dance, and Vera McNiff, the director of drama. Similar to schools operated today, lessons were provided after school and on Saturdays, and each lesson ran from one to two hours each. For the enjoyment of the students' parents, and to showcase their progress, special programs and recitals were offered periodically. Noel's very first public

THE EARLY YEARS

Minneapolis, 1927

The Sick Doll, 1925

performance was in *The Sick Doll* in 1925. A drama, it was performed at Norway Hall in Minneapolis. Noel had the lead role.

Noel continued with her studies in both dancing and drama at Seton Guild until 1930. During this five-year span, she seemed to have been in every production imaginable. At the same time, she nurtured her natural skill at dancing, which began with ballet lessons and later evolved into what was then called "specialty dancing," and sometimes later referred to as modern dance. She showed a particular talent for "Spanish dancing," which she perfected at eight years of age, and began featuring in school productions, private engagements, and in vaudeville. Later, tap dancing became her forte, with techniques learned at the Knickerbocker School of Dance.

It was also during this time that Noel made her first of many broadcasts over local radio. In October of 1928, Noel and LaVere walked into the studios of WDGY in Minneapolis. Over live radio, Noel calmly

Knickerbocker Dance Studio, 1930

RKO Orpheum Theatre with Jerry Levine and Randolph Norris, 1931

THE EARLY YEARS

Noel at age 8

THE EARLY YEARS

and confidently recited the story of *The Punishment of Mary Louise*, for the Children's Play Hour. Unfortunately, the recitation was not recorded, so the only copies that exist remain in the memories of the listeners of that day. This once-a-week children's broadcast was a popular favorite with children of her age. To be chosen to be a part of the show was akin to being in the peanut gallery of *Howdy Doody* or picked to be a contestant on one of today's Nickelodeon programs. Both children and adults alike either read or performed works that were both well-known, or obscure. Many of the performers even recited their own written words or plays during the life of this program. In the months and years to follow, Noel would become almost a regular feature on radio broadcasts nationwide, either as a single performer, a musical group member, or in recent years, an interviewee after a lifetime of work in the field of entertainment.

Noel Neill's first professional performance before a paying audience was in the 1930 vaudeville production of *Kid Nite Follies* billed as a "miniature musical comedy." She performed at the RKO Orpheum Theatre in Minneapolis with friends Jerry Levine (one of her two long-time dance partners; the other being Randy Norris); Billy Stonebreaker; and the Woodard Sisters. All were students of the Knickerbocker School. As a team, they gave a highly polished and professional show just before the screening of the film, *She's My Weakness*, starring Sue Clark and Arthur Lake (later to perform as film's "Dagwood"). The other acts on the bill were Pat Henning, Sidney Tracey, Bessie Hay, The Liazeed Troupe, and comedians Nelson Clifford and Marie Wilson. By this time already seasoned performers, Noel and the group were asked back time and again for shows at the Orpheum not only for evening programs, but for the well-attended matinees.

Later billed as the "Knickerbocker Kiddie Review," the "RKO Kiddie Revue," or "The Oriole Review," these shows were designed by heavyset comedian and master of ceremonies Larry Rich. Rich later

With Dance Partner, Randolph Norris, 1931

"Kid Nite Follies," 1930

THE EARLY YEARS

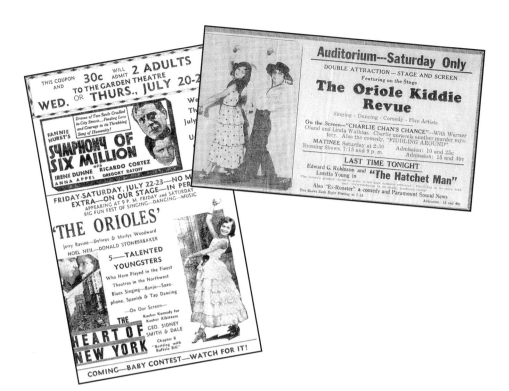

August, 1931

promoted singer and dancer Baby Rose Marie, who went on to even greater fame as the wise-cracking "Sally" on the popular 1960's sitcom, *The Dick Van Dyke Show*. Rich promoted Baby Rose Marie during her 1932 national tour of RKO theatres. In fact, Rich sent a letter to Rose Marie earlier in the year introducing Noel Neill. Handwritten on the letterhead of Boston's Hotel Metropolitan, he wrote:

"Dear Baby,
This will introduce little Noel Neill, a little friend of mine who is a charming little dancer. She will be glad to show you around the city of Minneapolis."

Noel and her mother did, indeed, escort Rose Marie around town. Although they talked of performing together, they never seemed to get that opportunity. Rose Marie stayed but a few days, then she was off

Baby Rose Marie, 1932
Minneapolis, MN

Promoter Larry Rich, 1932

THE EARLY YEARS

to another city. They did not meet again until October 13, 2002 at the 19th Annual Hollywood Reunion in Studio City, California – 70 years later. Also at the Hollywood reunion was singer Patty Andrews of the famous singing Andrews Sisters. Andrews confirmed that both she and Noel had attended the Knickerbocker School at the same time, had practiced together, and had actually performed together as youngsters at several of the RKO Orpheum theatres across Minnesota. But as she and her sisters were slightly older, they generally worked with an older group of singers and dancers for Larry Rich. Noel recalls the sisters vividly:

"The Andrew Sisters were from the north end of town, while I attended school in south Minneapolis. Since we attended the same dance school, we were good friends, and we seemed to have the same interests. Of the three sisters, I was closer in age to Patty, who also seemed to be the friendlier of the three. Even back then, the girls were seen as being very talented. Their father once hitched a ride with Mother and me when we drove to Denver one weekend. He slept in the back seat whenever we stopped for the night. These were the lean years for the Andrews family, and he was traveling west to drum up work for the girls. He later made his way to Los Angeles."

In between her engagements at the Orpheum and other theatres, Noel also managed to find dramatic stage work with the Bainbridge Players, with prominent roles in *The Magic Mill, Mrs. Wiggs Of The Cabbage Patch*, and *Snow White & The Seven Dwarfs*, all performed at Minneapolis' Shubert Theatre. In addition, she also performed with three-time Olympic Figure Skating Champion Gillis Grafstrom at the Minneapolis Arena as part of the "Children Foursome" of the Figure Skating Club. A natural athlete, although only twelve years of age, Noel already excelled in swimming and ice skating. In the same year, she also managed to work in numerous department store fashion shows as both a model and a performer.

Although very successful as a singer and dancer, Noel also longed to be an athlete. She was beginning to feel as though she was missing out on what she believed was a normal childhood. Up to this point, she viewed her life as a series of rehearsals and performances. She began to see less and less of her friends and her sports activities became fewer and fewer. Clearly, LaVere knew what she wanted for Noel, but she apparently never spoke with her daughter about these desires.

"Mother was a typical stage mom who did everything to encourage me to stay in the theatre. I knew it was important to her to see me succeed, and I didn't want to disappoint her. I don't think she could see that as a young child, I had other needs. Although I did have fun performing, to me, it was not everything, but to Mother, it *was* everything. Back then you just did not question your parents. You did what they wanted you to do, as long as it was reasonable and legal. Although it was becoming less fun, I continued performing."

Bryant Junior High School, 1933

THE EARLY YEARS

Mound, MN, 1933

"Jerry and Ginger," 1935

By 1934, at almost fourteen years of age, Noel had changed her stage name to "Ginger O'Neill," in part to capitalize on the name of Ginger Rogers and to bring attention to the distinct shading of her bright red hair. She and Jerry Levine became a much-sought-after song and dance team – "Jerry & Ginger" – performing popular tunes of the day and "Spanish dancing." Some enterprising promoters even billed them as "Internationally Famous Troupers," although neither had barely ventured out of the Midwest. It was also at this time that Noel took up the banjo and joined the Woodard Sisters, which became the Woodard Trio. With Marles Woodard on saxophone, Dolores Woodard on banjo, and Noel also on banjo, they sang, danced, and performed unlike any other musical group of their day. Jerry & Ginger and The Woodard Trio often traveled together, performing at the same events. In 1934 alone, these young but eager entertainers played the Minnesota State Fair, Iowa State Fair, Wisconsin State Fair, and the Tri-State Fair, as well as many private clubs and theatres. In 1935, both groups joined "Miller's Jewels of 1935," a slightly older version of the "Kiddie Review" shows. This group performed together throughout the Midwest until 1937. The Woodard Trio alternately became "The Three Musical Woodards," and "The Three Woodards," They continued to tour together also until 1937. One year earlier, at the age of sixteen years, and from the urging of her classmates, Noel decided to try her hand as a solo vocalist.

THE EARLY YEARS

The Woodard Trio
1934

The Woodard Trio for
Miller's Jewels, 1935

Johnson & Dean and The Woodard Trio,
Wisconsin State Fair, 1935

On February 14, 1936, through a local contact, and accompanied by her mother, Noel made her professional solo singing debut at the Blue Ribbon Nite Club in Albuquerque, New Mexico. Billed as "Noel Neill – Miss Variety," she sang mostly torch songs of the era with the house band. Greatly encouraged by the audience's warm reception, she quickly began to pursue more solo work while in high school, eventually singing with the Jimmy Pidgeon Orchestra, Leonard Keller and His Orchestra, and Eddie Rames and His Music. All three orchestras were already very popular Midwestern bands. Ironically, by all accounts a highly professional singer, dancer and actress who had performed in the best locations with some of the best acts around, Noel never could seem to win a role in any of her high school plays!

Noel's final performance for Miller's Jewels came as a solo vocalist and dancer at the Benson Fair Celebration in Minnevaukan, North Dakota, on June 26, 1937. It would also be the last time she would be billed as "Ginger." Earlier in the year she performed solo at the Roxy Theatre in Minneapolis, and at

August, 1936

Albuquerque, New Mexico
February 14, 1936

THE EARLY YEARS

the same time, she was startled to receive a different type of attention by being elected "Queen of Market Week" in the twin cities.

In spite of the frenetic pace of her performance schedule throughout her entire childhood years, Noel's school work never seemed to suffer. A bright child, she somehow still managed to turn out superior coursework in her elementary years at Bancroft School. She still found time to participate in sports at Bryant Junior High, and to date young men at Central High. She was elected secretary of the student council at age fifteen, and published a short story, "Wallpaper" in the 1935 book, *Ventures*. She was the assistant business manager of the high school newspaper, and joined Quill & Scroll, the "International Honorary Society For High School Students." An excellent writer, Noel could easily have earned a living writing for any number of publications. She did, in fact, apply to the University of Minnesota as a journalism

Wisconsin State Fair
1935

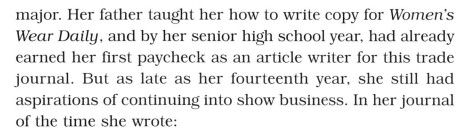

major. Her father taught her how to write copy for *Women's Wear Daily*, and by her senior high school year, had already earned her first paycheck as an article writer for this trade journal. But as late as her fourteenth year, she still had aspirations of continuing into show business. In her journal of the time she wrote:

"My one ambition is to be a dancer. When I'm through high school I hope to go to New York, or if not there, Chicago or California. Minneapolis is no town for anyone who seeks fame on the legitimate stage.

It seems that every little girl always wants to be a nurse and many still have that ambition when they grow up. I never gave it a second thought because I was so determined to be a dancer and I still have that idea, and that one goal in front of me."

Noel never did make it to the University of Minnesota, but she did later become the most recognized newspaper reporter the world would ever know – and a great little dancer. ★

David Neill, 1935

THE EARLY YEARS

Chapter 2:
Noel Neill, Songbird!

NOEL NEILL, SONGBIRD!

Minneapolis, 1938

With Sid Luft, Phoenix, AZ, 1938

After graduating from high school in January of 1938, Noel and her mother (whom she called "Tiny") embarked on a planned three-month-long automobile journey to both California and Mexico, visiting friends and relatives along the way. After a brief stay in Denver to see her cousins, they stopped in Phoenix to renew old friendships. Some friends from Minneapolis had built several cottages for rent alongside the road. Noel met very interesting characters while there:

"The cottages were close to a military base and one of the fellows receiving flight training was Sid Luft, later to become a movie producer. Sid talked about how he was going to go to Hollywood to make lots of money. I wasn't sure if he was trying to convince me or convince himself. But he did go to Hollywood, he did make lots of money, and he ended up marrying Judy Garland.

There was another fellow – 'Elmer' – who didn't seem to have a last name. I told him I was a singer and he said he knew the people who ran *Omar's Dome* in Los Angeles and that he could get me a job there. Well, people would tell you a lot of things to impress you, so I didn't put a lot of stock into what he was saying. But later, when I called him, he did get me the job, and not only that, he set it up so that some studio bigwigs were there to see me sing."

After Phoenix, Noel and LaVere then headed West to California and briefly rented an apartment in Los Angeles. Noel suddenly felt very much at home in California. Unlike Minnesota it was mostly warm year-round and she especially loved the ocean; she was so drawn to it that it was suddenly difficult for her to leave. The ocean breeze beckoned her and she gave in to its relentless pull, eventually staying almost ten months. Noel did not quite make it to Mexico on this trip, but she did find far more adventure than she had anticipated.

NOEL NEILL, SONGBIRD!

Within days of being in Los Angeles, Noel received a tip from her new next door neighbor, who worked for CBS, that the *Hotel Del Mar* in Del Mar, California was auditioning for a female singer. With little preparation, she rushed down for a quick audition, and to her surprise, she got the job! Noel and LaVere then quickly decided to move to Del Mar, so they rented a little cottage during the horse racing season. But she sang at the hotel for only a few days. On the evening of one of her first nights, Bing Crosby, who owned the *Del Mar Turf Club* across the street, heard Noel singing with the El Chancellor Band. He was so taken with her voice, her style, and her infectious smile, that he hired both Noel and the band to perform at the Turf Club the very next night. She successfully performed on weekends, Friday through Sunday, for two seasons, the summers of 1938 and 1939.

For a world-famous entertainer, Noel found Bing Crosby to be very accessible and very down-to-earth:

"Bing was very nice to me. I remember he was not too tall or too good-looking, but he was always very cordial and very upbeat. I didn't see him every night I worked because the place was always so packed with people coming for first the dinner shows, then for dancing. I do recall that once I wasn't feeling too well – it was earlier in the afternoon long before the shows – and Bing heard about it. He came up to me and said that he was going to have someone drive me to the beach house that he had nearby, and that his wife Dixie would fix me something. Well, we arrived, and obviously he had called her because she knew I was coming and she greeted me so warmly. She had the maid make me some herbal tea. We spent the rest of the afternoon chatting on her tennis court, while she was giving diction lessons to her twin boys who had speech problems. She was a wonderful person who was very kind and caring. I saw her a few times after that and she was always very kind to me."

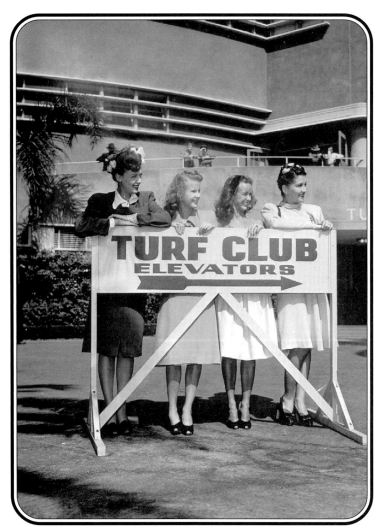

Del Mar Turf Club, 1939

For a veteran of dozens of musical performances as a child, singing ballads at the Turf Club was not difficult work. She started her first set at 9:00 p.m. for one hour, then commenced her second set at 10:30 p.m. Often she did not arrive back home to her shared cottage until well after 1:00 a.m. The next day she would sleep late, then head to the beach for an afternoon of sunbathing and surfing. Interestingly, along with a handful of other beachcombers, Noel soon became known as one of the original California surfers of this era, riding the waves on those heavy wooden boards of the day. Although most attention has been given to the male surfers of the 1930s for popularizing the sport, the ladies were equally as influential and Noel was at the forefront of this group. Several members of this very same group also pioneered beach volleyball in Santa Monica, with Noel being recognized as a world-class athletic competitor well into her 40s – despite being only

NOEL NEILL, SONGBIRD!

Noel Neill with Bing Crosby
Del Mar, California, 1938

NOEL NEILL, SONGBIRD!

5'2" tall, and weighing a mere 98 pounds. She was an unlikely athletic force to contend with, until you played against her!

The summer of 1938 also found Noel at the studios of Paramount Pictures. At the urging of LaVere, she applied for acting work. She knew that she could act, sing, and dance, but she silently wondered – was she good enough for the movies? Being a minor (not quite 18 yet) she not only needed her mother's written permission to work, but also her birth certificate and high school diploma. A quick call to Dad back in Minneapolis brought both items (accompanied by her last report card) in short order, via US Air Mail. David Neill, by this time News Editor of the *Minneapolis Star-Tribune,* was not too enthused about his only daughter entering the motion picture field. He thought she should have chosen a profession more financially safe and secure, like newspaper reporting. However, he never directly voiced a negative thought about her career choices. Eventually (but grudgingly) he would just go along with her stated desires and try not to get in the way.

But after receiving final approval of her application to work, Noel had second thoughts about working in motion pictures. She took a long hard look around her and realized that there was a lot of competition from other girls her age. But she also knew that she had a great job with Bing that other performers would have loved to have had. So she decided to focus on her singing, knowing that plenty of high-powered studio heads and celebrities frequented the club nightly. It would later prove to be one of the best decisions she would ever make in her career.

Toward the end of the racing season of 1938, Noel found another job singing – courtesy of "Elmer" – at a Los Angeles nightclub called *Omar's Dome*, a swanky night spot with a packed house every night. This venue gave her an opportunity to try different styles of music such as jazz. She sang her heart out for a full month before moving on to another nightclub across town, the *Somerset House*, where she sang until the end of the year. Most of the clientele of the *Somerset House* were the executive type, many of whom were the top brass at The May Company, a department store institution on Wilshire Boulevard. Noel remembers an encounter with the head of The May Company one night:

Ray Merrill & His Aristocrats, 1940

NOEL NEILL, SONGBIRD!

"As usual, I was singing away, and during the break he asked if I would like to work in the store during the day. It sounded like a good idea at the time. I worked there for only a few weeks as a sales lady, until I got my first paycheck, when pennies rolled out of the envelope. That didn't last very long."

The winter of 1939 found Noel back home in Minnesota, just in time for New Year's celebrations – and to ponder her future. Although only eighteen years old, she felt she needed to make a firm decision about her life. She had already spent most of her entire life in show business, and she was emotionally exhausted from years of practicing and performing. While she loved writing, the prospect of spending cold winters in snowy Minnesota did not hold enormous appeal, either. But she remembered the line in her journal about seeking the legitimate stage. So she went with her heart – and the pull of the ocean.

In March of 1939, Noel returned to California.

After a few quick telephone calls to several musician friends, Noel was able to secure yet another job as a solo vocalist, this time with Jimmy Walsh & His Orchestra at the *Mark Hopkins Hotel* in San Francisco. Again, she sang every night for almost a month, gaining more confidence with every song. At the conclusion of her obligation, she raced back to Del Mar, California for the beginning of the 1939 season at the *Del Mar Turf Club*. She believes she would have stayed longer in San Francisco had the weather not been unusually cold for that month.

As before, Noel was warmly received by the audiences at the Turf Club. After her stint at the club ended, Noel was considered a professional singer with enviable range – although she was still only eighteen years old. She and Bing Crosby became friends, and she sounded, acted, and danced as a much older veteran singer of ballads, jazz and swing, yet she looked younger than her eighteen years. She had her pick of singing jobs, but, again, she went back home to Minneapolis for the winter to relax and to see her family.

Mark Hopkins Hotel, San Francisco, 1939

NOEL NEILL, SONGBIRD!

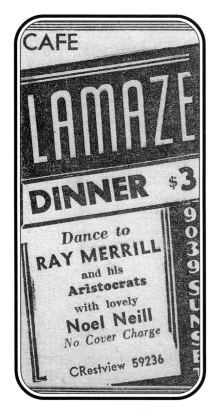

Santa Rita Hotel, Tucson, AZ, 1940

Noel's time at home lasted barely a month before she accepted an offer to sing with Ray Merrill & His Aristocrats at the trendy *Cafe Lamaze* on Sunset Strip in Beverly Hills in February of 1940. This engagement led to yet another job with the same orchestra at the historic *Santa Rita Hotel* in Tucson, Arizona. It was while in Tucson that Noel once again began to think about appearing in motion pictures when she stumbled across the crew filming the Bill Holden Western, *Arizona*.

After a few minutes of watching the actors work, a wave of cold chills suddenly swept across her body, and Noel sensed – she knew – that her life was only just beginning. ★

Santa Rita Hotel, Tucson, AZ, 1940

Chapter 3:
You Ought To Be In Pictures!

YOU OUGHT TO BE IN PICTURES

Being in Tucson, Arizona in the middle of the summer can be a brutal and unrewarding experience. For many locals, the day does not begin until the sun goes down. For the crew of *Arizona,* filming in the hot mid-day sun in 1940, nighttime brought welcome relief to an unbelievable day of blistering heat with temperatures well above 100 degrees. One of the hot spots for entertainment was the nightclub located within the now-historic *Santa Rita Hotel*. On one particular night the publicist for the studio decided to visit the club with several members of the crew. Ray Merrill and His Aristocrats was the featured band and Noel Neill, the featured singer. After the first set, the publicist invited Noel to the set of *Arizona*, which was filming in the desert just outside of town. She arrived early the next day eager to learn all she could about motion pictures. The publicist quickly took her around the dusty set and introduced her to several members of the cast and crew. Finally, they visited the stables where the wranglers kept the horses and it was here that Noel was invited to sit atop the beautiful painted pony that star Bill Holden rode in this classic Western. Intrigued by what he saw, the publicist hastily called for the studio photographer, who quickly shot several frames of what would later prove to be the very first of hundreds of publicity stills of Noel. Although she never appeared in this film, these amazing photographs circulated around Paramount and other studios for several years, eventually serving to promote her as a Western film star.

Following her Tucson engagement at the *Santa Rita Hotel*, Noel rushed back to California and a new apartment in Los Angeles. Now more than ever, motion pictures were on her mind and she decided to pursue film work with the same full fury that she had tackled all of her endeavors. She contacted Bing Crosby's agent, his brother Ernie, for representation.

Unfortunately, the answer he gave her was one she did not want to hear:

"Ernie was a very bright man and a very good agent. However, he felt he would have a conflict if he had tried to represent me. He said, 'Noel, I would love to be your agent. But I'm Susan Hayward's agent. You look so much alike that I fear you'll be competing for the same parts. Since I started with her first, it's only right that I stay with her.' While I didn't really care for his answer, I did appreciate his candor.

Hollywood, 1941

The Brown Derby Restaurant
Hollywood, CA, 1940

YOU OUGHT TO BE IN PICTURES

On the set of *Arizona*, 1940

YOU OUGHT TO BE IN PICTURES

He wished me luck and off I went. Ironically, a few years later (1947) Susan and I did eventually work together in *Smash-Up, The Story Of A Woman*. She was wonderful in the lead role as a neglected wife and I was glad to have worked with her."

A little discouraged, but certainly not giving up, Noel continued singing at small clubs on the weekends and hitting the phones the rest of the week. Her perseverance finally paid off when she arranged to meet with agent Jack Pomeroy at the *Brown Derby Restaurant* in Hollywood. Pomeroy had actually seen Noel perform at the Turf Club and expressed surprise that another agent had not yet approached her. They quickly agreed to an agents's fee of 10%, with the arrangement being wholly verbal. During the next eight years that Jack Pomeroy acted on her behalf, their arrangement always operated on a handshake basis. Pomeroy later also represented actor Jack Larson, best known as TV's Jimmy Olsen.

Pomeroy found Noel work in a minor, uncredited role in her first film, Monogram's *Henry Aldrich For President* (1941) starring Jimmy Lydon. She had several brief scenes as a student and did well enough that she was hired for a similar part in *Miss Polly* (1941). Three additional Henry Aldrich films followed, each with expansive, credited roles in *Henry & Dizzy* (1942), *Henry Rocks The Cradle* (1943), and *Henry Aldrich's Little Secret* (1944). Noel's characters in these films offered sharp-tongued dialogue to usually dim-witted accomplices. In between the Aldrich films were small parts in Shirley Temple's

With Jimmy Lydon & June Preisser
Henry Aldrich For President, 1941

Henry & Dizzy, 1942

YOU OUGHT TO BE IN PICTURES

The Gopher Theatre, Minneapolis, 1942

Miss Annie Rooney (1942), *Salute For Three* (1943), and the Hal Roach comedy *Prairie Chickens* (1943) starring Noah Berry, Jr., who was known off-stage as "Pidge." But it was a dancing showgirl part

With Jimmy Rogers, son of Will Rogers, *Prairie Chickens*, 1943

YOU OUGHT TO BE IN PICTURES

Prairie Chickens, 1943

YOU OUGHT TO BE IN PICTURES

With Michael O'Shea
Lady of Burlesque, 1943

With Pinky Lee
Lady of Burlesque, 1943

in *Lady Of Burlesque* (1943) that landed Noel her first big studio contract. Within the first five minutes of this film Noel takes center stage in a chorus line routine that first displays her now-trademark smile and that unique twinkle in her eyes. The bosses at Paramount were so taken by the charisma of this little dancer that they immediately signed her to their standard seven-year contract – without the usual screen test.

At $75 per week, Noel Neill was well on her way to becoming one of the busiest actresses in pictures. One of her first films under this contract was *The Road To Utopia* (1944) with Bob Hope and her old friend, Bing Crosby. On her very first day back on the Paramount lot, Noel and Bing ran into one another quite by accident:

"I had just arrived on the lot and was on my way to the set when I heard someone behind me singing the Christmas tune, *Noel*. I turned around and there was "Der Bingle," as happy as can be, riding a bicycle across the lot. He asked if everything was going well for me and I replied that it was. Then he said, 'If anyone ever gives you any trouble, just let me or my brother Ernie know, and we'll take care of it.' Bing was so protective of me and I knew that his words were genuine. I never needed his help, but it was comforting to know that he was there for me if I needed him."

YOU OUGHT TO BE IN PICTURES

Over The Santa Fe Trail, 1947

Thus began what eventually would total eighty-nine films. From 1941 to 2002, Noel Neill starred in just about every type of film that has ever been made, from comedies to mysteries to documentaries. Of her extensive catalog of films, Westerns stand out as her most frequently visited genre, having acted in thirteen Western feature films and two Western movie serials. Of this collection, only *Over The Santa Fe Trail* (1947) managed to almost fully showcase her stage skills.

A musical-comedy starring Ken Curtis as one of the last of the singing cowboys, Noel played the spirited role of a singing medicine show performer with the ironic name of "Taffy Neill." *Over The Santa Fe Trail* was her first Western and Noel jumps into this role full-force with wonderful comedic timing, a beautiful singing voice, and a great stage presence. The only thing missing was her well-honed tap dancing. Years later, memory of Ken Curtis as a singing cowboy would be largely forgotten as he took on the role of "Festus" in TV's *Gunsmoke* opposite James Arness. Only after the show's incredible twenty-year network run did Curtis reacquaint the world with his superb singing voice, as he played dozens of state and county fairs and dinner theatres until his death in 1991.

YOU OUGHT TO BE IN PICTURES

Gun Runner, 1948

With Whip Wilson, *Abilene Trail,* 1949

Another cowboy singing co-star was Jimmy Wakely. In *Gun Runner* (1948) Noel and Jimmy worked together to dwarf a gang of criminals from illegally selling guns to renegades. In this, and most of her other Western appearances, Noel was primarily cast in the leading female role as the daughter or niece of a rancher who is being tricked or cheated into selling his land. The leading man is usually the wandering honest stranger who happens to be riding through town on his way to a better life.

This storyline is repeated over and again in *Gun Runner, Abilene Trail* (1949) with Whip Wilson, *Marshall's Reward* (1951), and *Whistling Hills* (1951) with legendary cowboy star Johnny Mack Brown. *Whistling Hills* was one of Brown's last cowboy features, having made his film debut in 1927s *Slide Kelly Slide*, after an incredible college football career at the University of Alabama resulting in the MVP award at the Rose Bowl in 1926.

Johnny Mack Brown in *Whistling Hills* co-starring Jimmy Ellison with Noel Neill, Lee Roberts, & Marshall Reed, 1951

Abilene Trail, 1949

YOU OUGHT TO BE IN PICTURES

YOU OUGHT TO BE IN PICTURES

Abilene Trail, 1949

Abilene Trail, 1949

The role of the daughter or niece was one that held two sides: she was either the helpless obedient waif in matronly dress or the assertive and aggressive gun-toting heroine. Of the former, that role was played to the hilt in *Gun Runner*, as Noel gazed lovingly into Jimmy Wakely's eyes as he serenaded her on horseback along the dusty trail. Of the latter, Noel was never better than in *Son Of A Badman* (1949) with Lash LaRue. She goes toe to toe with the Lash as she upstages him in every scene. Evidently comfortable in boots, pants, fancy shirt and hat, Noel rides horseback with ease and gives the impression that no man is her equal.

Producers just did not seem to know exactly what to do with female Western stars, so they were more often than not typed into one of these two categories. But on a rare occasion, such as in *Whistling Hills* they would play both parts, but with a twist: playing both a very good girl in girlish attire, and a very bad woman in cowgirl dress.

The same themes were also carried over in the movie serials of the 1940s. In both *The Adventures of Frank & Jesse James* (1948) with Clayton Moore and *The James Brothers Of Missouri* (1949) with Keith Richards, Noel often found herself helplessly tied to a chair awaiting the fate of her sweetheart Jesse James. Clayton would soon be tied to his own character as *The Lone Ranger*, a role he rode to

The Adventures Of Frank & Jesse James
1948

With Keith Richards
The James Brothers Of Missouri, 1949

YOU OUGHT TO BE IN PICTURES

Over The Santa Fe Trail, 1947

YOU OUGHT TO BE IN PICTURES

With Eddie Foy, Jr., *Fun Time*, 1944

the end of his days in 1999. Noel and Clayton would eventually meet again (and for the last time on screen) in 1951 in a television episode of *The Lone Ranger*, "Letter Of The Law."

Although Noel's greatest body of work was in Westerns, other film genre filled her screen time, namely, "*The Teenagers*" series at Monogram, several shorts at Paramount, various Superman films, the last Charlie Chan feature, and many war-time era comedies, musicals, mysteries, and dramas.

One of the methods studios used to showcase their rising stars was to cast them in small two-reelers, known as "shorts." These films usually ran only about twenty minutes and were projected just before the main feature film, or between a double-feature. Several stars of the 1930s and 1940s – such as Laurel & Hardy and The Three Stooges – gained their fame from primarily this form of entertainment. Noel starred in four such shorts: *Fun Time* (1944) with Eddie Foy, Jr. (filmed in Technicolor and nominated for an Academy Award for its photography); *Caribbean Romance* (1944) a plotless wonder, again with Jimmy Lydon; *You Hit The Spot* (1945); and *College Queen* (1945) with Jim Phelan. All were musicals, and with the exception of *Caribbean Romance*, Noel had the female lead in each. *College Queen*, in particular, was a standout role for Noel. Almost a rags to riches tale, Noel plays a hard-working college student with a night waitressing job in the campus malt shop, who is chosen to be the dance partner in a song and dance routine. She and her partner win the competition as Noel sports a high alto in singing "The Old Oak Trail" and tap dances across the screen in high heels. A well-choreographed number, the director effectively chooses between a combination of master shots and close-ups, and for once we are finally offered a brief glimpse of what Noel could do on a stage. She bounces, taps, glides, and smiles her way through this difficult routine, and while she performs, all

YOU OUGHT TO BE IN PICTURES

eyes are on her. Unfortunately, *College Queen* would be the last short she would ever make, but this performance did gain the attention of other studios.

As a contract player, Noel Neill was subject to being loaned out to other studios, which occurred frequently. In fact, from 1943 to 1950 (the length of her contract), almost one-third of her films were made for studios other than Paramount. One such loan was to Sam Katzman, who was an old-time independent producer and director whose career dated back to the silent era. He had a reputation for coming in on budget and more than 90% of his films made money. Katzman was casting for a series of *"Teenagers"* films for Monogram, similar to the Henry Aldrich series, but with a high school setting. He had seen Noel Neill in *College Queen* and the Aldrich series, and thought she would be perfect for his ensemble cast.

From 1945 to 1948, *"The Teenagers"* series produced nine feature films, all completed quickly, under budget, and all very profitable. With co-stars Freddie Stewart, June Preisser, Frankie Darro, Warren Mills, and Donald MacBride, Noel was chosen to play the same role in the entire series, that of 16-year-old Betty Rogers, the high school newspaper editor. With large round black glasses, she looked and acted every bit of the part, although when production on the first film started (*Junior Prom* 1945) she was already 25-years-old. By the time the series was completed in 1948, she was 28-years-old. This is also the same year that Noel made her greatest number of films – an astounding fifteen films in less than twelve months!

Toward the end of *"The Teenagers"* run, Katzman again cast Noel in her first movie serial of 15 chapters, *Brick Bradford* (1947). She played Lula, a native girl. This role was followed by three additional serials: *The Adventures of Frank & Jesse James* (1948); the phenomenally successful Superman serials: *Superman* (1948) and *Atom Man Vs. Superman* (1950), both with Kirk Alyn; and *The James Brothers Of Missouri* (1949). Harry Cohn, head of Columbia Studios, would later remark that the Superman serials quite literally saved Columbia from bankruptcy during those difficult years.

The Teenagers in *Smart Politics*, 1948

Superman - The Serial, 1948

YOU OUGHT TO BE IN PICTURES

Sky Dragon, 1951

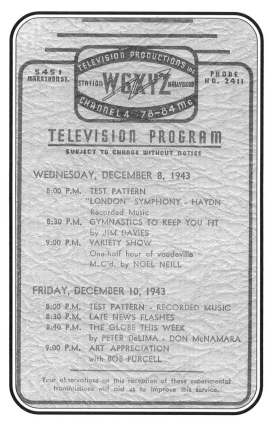

In March of 1950, Noel was at the end of her Paramount contract and she had one more film to complete for the studio, that being the last in the very long series of Charlie Chan films, *Sky Dragon* (1950), with Roland Winters in the title role. With the wrap of this production, Noel had starred in an unbelievable sixty-one films under her Paramount contract. But there were other distinctions in Noel's career that few film historians have noted.

In 1943, at the very beginning of her stint with Paramount Pictures, Noel discovered that the studio had a television show on the lot. The concept of television was so new that the studio bosses were not aware of its existence. Spearheaded by television broadcast pioneer Klaus Landsberg, it has been argued that this project was the first such studio in Hollywood. Noel remembers these days with fondness:

"During my first days at Paramount, there was a rumor going around about Klaus renting one of the older stages with the rundown dressing rooms. I wandered over there one day to see what was going on and found Klaus, in his normal rough and gruff manner, ordering the Paramount mail room kids about. They, too, had heard about this thing called television and everyone seemed to want to be a part of it. Klaus trained them to use the cameras and other equipment in exchange for free help. I hadn't quite started in any great roles yet, so I volunteered to MC the very first television program there. It was called *Variety Show* and ran on WGXYZ on Channel 4 in Hollywood. It was billed as "one-half hour of vaudeville," and it ran from 9:00 p.m. to 9:30 p.m. In addition to MC, I sang, danced, and even did an exercise program, long before Jack Lalanne took his program to

WGXYZ-TV *Variety Show* Exercise Program, 1943

YOU OUGHT TO BE IN PICTURES

national audiences. Klaus brought in other acts to perform, and this idea was so new, he didn't pay them, either. The only TV sets in the area at the time were at the Douglas Aircraft plant, so Klaus sold commercial air time to them. Douglas, in turn, made televisions available to their employees to watch during the dinner hour for the night shift."

Noel continued with *Variety Hour* until her movie-making hours began taking more and more of her time. She reluctantly gave up her television job for the demands of the bigger screen that began to include other duties, as well.

Almost immediately after signing her studio contract, the Paramount publicity machine shifted into high gear with calculated press releases, photo opportunities at arranged personal appearances, war bond rallies, and professionally photographed movie stills and lavish portraits. Noel suddenly found herself in the middle of an almost chaotic cavalcade of publicity. But publicity was something Noel was

Paramount still, 1943

YOU OUGHT TO BE IN PICTURES

Paramount stills, 1943

YOU OUGHT TO BE IN PICTURES

Hollywood, 1940

YOU OUGHT TO BE IN PICTURES

WWII GI Pinup, 1943

YOU OUGHT TO BE IN PICTURES

Print advertisement for auto wax, using Noel's very own Packard convertible, 1944

Here Come The Waves
1944

Rainbow Island, 1944

already very familiar with much of her life and she well-understood that often facts were exaggerated to fit a circumstance and engagements were announced to promote an upcoming film project. So it came as no surprise that she was also asked to pose for what was then called "Leg Art," the style of photography that accentuated the lower extremities of the female body. The best example of leg art is the now-famous Betty Grable photograph of her looking back over her right shoulder, with focus squarely on her backside and legs. This photograph would eventually become the most requested pinup by American GIs during the early 1940s. What is generally not known is that the photograph of Noel leaning back onto the rocks at Will Rogers State Beach in Santa Monica, was the second-most requested pinup by GIs during the second world war. Paramount publicists were immediately taken by surprise by this instant response and Noel was rushed into film after film to capitalize on this sudden wave of interest. In 1944 alone, she appeared in thirteen separate film projects, starting with minor roles in films such as *Rainbow Island*, to major parts in the popular *Here Come The Waves* (again, with Bing) and the critically-acclaimed social commentary, *Are These Our Parents?* Although *Here Come The Waves* was a great opportunity to play opposite her friend Bing and to have the second female lead to Betty Hutton, the script called for Noel to cut her long red hair down to a short Navy cut. Up until that time, her hair was always long and she feared the change might negatively alter her screen persona. Her fears were for naught, as her popularity continued to soar after the film's release. Throughout the remainder of her career, her hair length never again became an issue of concern.

YOU OUGHT TO BE IN PICTURES

Are These Our Parents?, 1944

Are These Our Parents? was an unusual success in a sea full of entertainment films. Released at a time when war was still being waged in Europe, North Africa, and Japan, expectation for its fate were generally low. Moviegoers were used to being entertained by comedies and musicals, which were seen as morale boosters and pick-me-ups. Then along comes this little well-acted Monogram film on alcoholism and parental misbehavior and irresponsibility and audiences suddenly are pushed into remembering that there are still problems right at home to be dealt with. This film, quite literally, opened the door for Ray Milland's *The Lost Weekend* (1945). The reviews at the time took particular notice of Noel Neill, generally stating that her role as a delinquent teenager was steeped in convincing realism. A reviewer for the *Los Angeles Times* wrote "A truly vivid character study is that of the younger girl, and the role is brilliantly played by Noel Neill, whose emotional reactions are startlingly effective. She looks like a young Katherine Hepburn."

Noel carried that wave of movie stardom all the way to the end of her contract, after which, like so many others, she simply became an independent contractor, acting in an additional eighteen films from 1951 to 1954. It was also during this time that Noel began her unparalleled reign as one of the most beloved television characters the world would know – the indomitable Lois Lane.

In looking back on her film career, Noel mused about what might have been:

"Not unlike any other profession, I had my ups and downs in the picture business. Although I did somehow manage to make a lot of films, I probably could have made many more, and been a bigger

YOU OUGHT TO BE IN PICTURES

With Alan Hale, Jr. in *Music Man*, 1947

When My Baby Smiles At Me, 1948

Victor Mature & Betty Hutton, 1949

star, had I not spent so much time at the beach. Back when my Paramount contract began, I would run in, say my lines, then head to the beach. It was almost a daily ritual for me. I'm sure I missed a few choice jobs and missed working with some great actors, but in retrospect, I truly have no regrets. Often when one looks back at their life, you wonder whether a decision one way or the other would have changed life's direction. In 1947, I met Victor Mature on the Paramount lot. He asked me to go to Las Vegas with him for the weekend. At first I said yes, but between the time I said yes and the next morning when he came to pick me up, I thought it over and wondered what in the world I was thinking at the time! So when he arrived, I told him I had changed my mind and would not be going. He was fine with that and went happily on his way. But years later I wondered how my life would have changed had I not changed my mind. He was likeable and well-spoken and such a happy-go-lucky fellow – but I just didn't run off with strangers, no matter how good-looking they were. I believe that in life we have choices and that we live and die by those choices. I also believe there is really nothing wrong with having regrets, but I think we also have to be accepting of our choices and live life as best we can." ★

YOU OUGHT TO BE IN PICTURES

Paramount still, 1944

Chapter 4:
Up, Up, & Away!
Superman – The Serials

UP, UP, & AWAY! SUPERMAN – THE SERIALS!

*I*n 1948, after seven years of starring in more than forty films for mostly Paramount Pictures, Noel Neill was offered the role of "Lois Lane" in the 15-Chapter Serial, *Superman*. In this Sam Katzman production for Columbia Pictures, Noel was given the role without having to audition for the part. Having already appeared in several Katzman productions such as *Brick Bradford*, Katzman already knew what he had in the talented Miss Neill. Physically, Noel strongly resembled the character in the comic books, and her lively, funny, self-assured, yet competitive performance as "Lois Lane" gave life and depth to the generally one-dimensional comic book character.

Superman was not only a live action adventure, but also one of the very first science fiction adventures to hit the screen. After the success of the comic books, the wonderful cartoon series by Max Fleischer, and the popular radio program with Bud Collyer, Columbia was given the go-ahead to develop a new screen version of the popular hero. A script was hastily prepared that pitted the "visitor from another planet" against the sinister "Spider Lady." Played by Carol Forman, "Spider Lady" attempts to take over the world by using a mysterious "relativity reducer ray" aimed at Metropolis. Equally as mysterious was the "Spider Lady's" unusual accent of undetermined origin. The role of "Jimmy Olsen, Cub Reporter" was energetically played by former *Little Rascals* star, Tommy Bond. Pierre Watkin played the loud and cantankerous "Perry White," editor of the *Daily Planet*. Watkin would later show up in several episodes of the television version, usually in a character role.

With a budget of $350,000 – at the time the largest ever for a serial – Sam Katzman wanted to make a true, live action adventure unlike any other. He would not be disappointed in the results. For the dual roles of "Clark Kent/Superman" he tapped the relatively unknown 37 year-old actor, Kirk Alyn. Although he had already worked for Katzman in six films, Alyn still was required to audition for the role. He was stunned to learn that at least 20 actors had already auditioned for the part weeks prior to his audition with the producer. And before meeting with Katzman, he had to pass the approval of several officials from National Comics Syndicate – the owners of the *Superman* trademark. Years later, Noel Neill would remark that of the three main actors to play the Man of Steel (Kirk Alyn, George Reeves, and Christopher Reeve), Alyn was the most athletic of the trio. Initially a stage actor and dancer, Kirk Alyn

With Kirk Alyn in *Superman*, 1948

Pierre Watkin, Kirk Alyn, Noel Neill, & Tommy Bond, *Superman*, 1948

On the set of *Superman*, 1948

(his real name was John Feggo) originally trained as a ballet dancer. During the late 1920s and early 1930s he worked in the New York vaudeville circuit, then starred on Broadway in several successful musicals and dramas. By the mid-1930s he made the leap to Hollywood to star in 1934's *Private Lessons*, where he was billed as "Jack Fago." Alyn's athleticism and dance background served him well for *Superman's* dual roles: he not only performed all of his own stunts with ease, but did so with a ballet dancer's dramatic flair. However, Noel also observed that Alyn was the most egotistical of the three "supermen." After filming, Alyn would often wear his hair with that little curl over his forehead as the *Superman* character did, and his boastful remarks to the press regarding his superhuman exploits on the set verged on bravado and embellishment.

The filming of *Superman* took six weeks to complete. Filming took place at Columbia's studios in Hollywood and location shots were completed in and around the Los Angeles area. Similar to every other Katzman production, rehearsals were few and completed shots were made in just one or two takes. This method left very little opportunity for detailed character development or refinement. Scenes were often filmed out of sequence, further blurring and confusing the actor's sense of story continuity. In addition, Sam Katzman was not averse to re-using the same scenes in the same film. Time after time the familiar scene of "Clark Kent" changing into "Superman" in the *Daily Planet* storeroom was used over and again. Further, clips from completed Katzman films can be seen in specialty shots that ordinarily would require expensive and expansive filming. For example, the rough airplane landing in Chapter 15

UP, UP, & AWAY! SUPERMAN – THE SERIALS!

of *Superman* is exactly the same footage that was used in Katzman's 1947 serial classic, *Jack Armstrong - All American Boy*, starring John Hart. Tommy Carr, the director of *Superman*, continued this legacy in filming television's highly popular *The Adventures of Superman*. As every George Reeves fan knows, almost every episode of this exciting television series contains scenes from past episodes.

At first, Noel Neill saw the role of "Lois Lane" as just another acting job, but soon realized that all was not what it appeared to be. Her life would soon change as never before.

Dressed in her trademark white wide-brimmed hat, woolen business suit, and with her long shoulder-length hair, Noel's low, distinct voice and no-nonsense delivery distinguished her from other actresses of this era. This role was uniquely different from other roles in other films. In fact, the only similar character of the 1940s was Rosalind Russell's "Hildy Johnson" in *His Girl Friday*. Both "Lois Lane" and "Hildy Johnson" dominate in male-oriented newspaper settings and both became feminist icons. When Noel smiled it was warm and loving and we smiled with her. But when she was angry or upset, it was quick, to the point, and thoroughly recognizable. There was never an instance when this "Lois" was coy or demure in her emotions. Much of this characterization might be due to the direction of Tommy Carr, who encouraged fast delivery and quick pacing. But Noel says that she simply played herself.

UP, UP, & AWAY! SUPERMAN – THE SERIALS!

If Noel Neill did, indeed, play herself, then what she played was what moviegoers wanted to see. Although "Superman" was the star of the show, "Lois Lane" was always there to make his life unpredictable and to meld together the continual confrontation between good and evil. More than a love interest, Noel became one of the best reasons to tune in every Saturday afternoon.

After its release in 1948, *Superman* quickly became one of the most watched – and one of the most profitable – serials in cinematic history, earning Columbia Pictures and National Comics millions of dollars in revenue. It became so successful that in 1949 National authorized Columbia to film fifteen chapters of a new series, *Atom Man Versus Superman*.

Released in 1950, *Atom Man Versus Superman* was the story of "warped genius" "Lex Luthor's" (Lyle Talbot) plans to conquer "Superman" and take over the world. Interior and street shots were filmed at Monogram's studios in Hollywood, and exterior location scenes were filmed at Corrigan's Ranch in the San Fernando Valley, the site of dozens of filmed Western features.

All the main characters from the first serial returned, so more cliff-hanging derring-do was guaranteed. Most of the sets – primarily the *Daily Planet* building and offices – remained as before, but Noel Neill's physical appearance had changed. Gone was the drab single woolen business suit and long hair. She now sported three very attractive outfits, and her hair was now much darker and considerably shorter. The wide-brimmed white hat was replaced with three smaller versions of varying colors.

UP, UP, & AWAY! SUPERMAN – THE SERIALS!

Atom Man Versus Superman, 1949
(Released in 1950)

Although quite active in the first serial, Noel found herself performing more demanding physical stunts in the sequel, so the changes in hats, suits and hair were made for practical purposes. Further, these changes tended to make her look slightly older, more physically mature, and more professional-looking as a reporter. Again, the same scenes of "Clark Kent" changing into "Superman" were re-used from the original. A rocket ship used in the last two chapters of *Superman* were again culled directly from 1947's *Jack Armstrong*. In an ironic twist, in Chapter 3 of *Atom Man*, John Hart has a small, non-speaking role as a hired thug, riding in the backseat of a large black sedan as it races across the countryside chasing an airplane. The airplane footage used in *Atom Man* is also the very same footage shown in *Jack Armstrong*, with John as the pilot. So in a very real sense, John Hart is apparently chasing himself!

Special effects were superior to the original, from the opening sequence of the atom bomb exploding, to "Superman" straddling a launched rocket (reminiscent of Slim Pickens riding the bomb in *Dr. Strangelove*). "Lex Luthor" also uses a device called a "space transporter" almost two decades before the appearance of a very similar transporter on TV's *Star Trek*. Earthquakes, floods, light rays, X-Ray machines, space travel, flying saucers, and collapsing buildings, all were featured in this rollicking sequel. But the one change that would have long-lasting effect was the new visual image of "Superman" flying.

In the first serial, and much of the second, when "Superman" flies, what we see is a filmed animation sequence. But in a few selected parts of *Atom Man*, Kirk Alyn is filmed in supposedly live-action flight.

UP, UP, & AWAY! SUPERMAN – THE SERIALS!

After repeated efforts to film Alyn hanging from wires failed, they simply filmed him standing still with his arms and hands pointing skyward. By turning the camera sideways and positioning a large fan directly over his head (to resemble rushing air in flight) and using a blue cyclorama as a sky backdrop, you have a very convincing image of "Superman" in flight! Not a new concept, this method has been utilized by every cinematographer since the beginning of moving pictures, but it remains an effective, inexpensive, and indispensable filmmaking tool.

Although both *Superman* and *Atom Man Versus Superman* were recognized as pioneering film projects back in 1948 and 1949, Noel had no desire to simply rest on the outcome of these two productions, so she continued acting in an amazing number of other films. In the same years of the two *Superman* serials, Noel Neill acted in an incredible 21 films. Her work can be found in everything from *Son Of A Badman* opposite Lash LaRue, to the last of the Charlie Chan films, *Sky Dragon*, to *The Adventures Of Frank & Jesse James*, with Clayton Moore, later to become *The Lone Ranger*. Years later, in the mid 1970's, at the beginning of the television and movie memorabilia craze, Clayton called Noel at home and asked what she knew about these "so-called autograph shows." He had heard that she had participated in a few events and he was interested in learning more about them. Noel and Clayton had always been good friends – had always liked working together at Republic – so she told him what they were all about, who to talk to, and how to get involved. Before long, Clayton Moore became a highly active signer of "Lone Ranger" memorabilia at special events nationwide and he continued doing these very popular shows until just a few years before his passing in December of 1999.

Noel was not too particular about what films she acted in. She had no grand illusions about the profession. She saw herself simply as an actress, and what actresses do is act, so she took what was offered, when it was offered, as long as it was from a legitimate studio. She simply liked to work. She believed that the more you worked, the more you were noticed, so the more work you were given. She would later tell me "In the old days it was not too hard to get an acting job. The studios made so many films back then that often it was just a matter of some casting director saying, 'Well, we could use a blonde or a brunette for the part,' and I was usually eager for the work. Plus, studios made money by loaning you out to other studios. If you were working on a big budget film and you had a few days off from filming, you could always get a couple of days work in a Western. I know that some of the bigger name actors and actresses looked down on Westerns, but I enjoyed doing them. I liked the settings, the talent was always top-notch, and the crews were great to work with. There was a certain camaraderie in Westerns that you didn't have in other film projects."

As expected, *Atom Man Versus Superman* was a huge hit for Columbia and National Comics. The serial enhanced the acting reputations of all involved in this production. Based on the strength of these two serials, National Comics quickly decided to further expand the role of "Superman" right into feature films. To the shock of everyone, Kirk Alyn had also decided he no longer wanted to portray the "Man of Steel." Although his reputation as an actor had been enhanced, he suddenly and quickly also found himself typecast as "Superman;" so much so that other work was becoming difficult to come by. Casting directors suddenly could not seem to see him as anything but "Superman." So he chose to "stop the bleeding" before his career was irreparably harmed. He returned to New York and made several other films and another serial, but for the remainder of his career he never achieved the same height of popularity that his role as "Superman" had attained. He never expressed a sense of regret or remorse over leaving the role that had made him famous.

UP, UP, & AWAY! SUPERMAN – THE SERIALS!

Noel Neill believes that since Kirk Alyn was so identified with the role of "Superman," National decided to re-cast all the major players from the serial, so there would be no confusion or comparison with the feature film. They simply wanted to start with a clean slate. Of course, Noel was hurt and felt a bit slighted by their decision, but she also saw herself as a professional, and was well aware that those things happened all the time in the film industry. So she moved on, making several other films such as *An American In Paris* with Gene Kelly, *Submarine Command* with Bill Holden, *Whistling Hills* opposite cowboy star Johnny Mack Brown, and *Gentlemen Prefer Blondes* with Marilyn Monroe and Jane Russell. Interestingly, in this last film, one of the best musical numbers Noel was ever in (a dance routine) was cut because Russell thought that the female dancers looked a bit too good, so it was re-shot with beefcake counterparts.

While Noel Neill was not part of the 1951 *Superman* feature film, she was not unhappy either. At age 30, she truly believed that the best of her career had yet to come. To millions of young television viewers all across America from 1953 to 1957, all seemed to be in total agreement, as she was about to embark on a lifelong journey of mythic proportions that continues to this day. ★

Scene deleted from *Gentlemen Prefer Blondes*

UP, UP, & AWAY! SUPERMAN – THE SERIALS!

With Cornel Wilde in
The Greatest Show On Earth, 1952

Chapter 5:
The Adventures Of Superman: The Television Years

THE ADVENTURES OF SUPERMAN: THE TELEVISION YEARS

At a time when studios were beginning to let go of most of their actors and actresses because of the sudden popularity of something new called "television," National Comics – solely on the strength of the two *Superman* serials – jumped into the feature film market anyway with 1951's *Superman & The Mole Men*. Several studios had already shut down completely and as Gary Grossman notes in his now classic groundbreaking book, *Superman: Serial to Cereal* (1976), why would anyone pay to see a show when you can see one for free! One person who was on the cusp of leading-man stardom was the young actor George Reeves. A veteran of many Western, gangster, and jungle films, dozens of stage performances, and like Noel, a Paramount contract player, George Reeves – who was born George Besselo – was offered the role of "Superman" after a quick audition. At first, he was not certain he wanted to play the "Man Of Steel." He was vaguely familiar with the character from the comic strip, but he saw himself as more of a romantic leading-man, not a flying savior of the world. However, roles in general were getting more scarce – much less leading-man roles – so he accepted the part with the reasoning that it was just a few weeks of work and he had played every other part, so "why not Superman."

But this production was not for a single feature film, it was for 26 episodes of a new television series titled *The Adventures of Superman*. The feature film, *Superman & The Mole Men*, released prior to the series, was simply a two-part episode from the series edited together, but released long before the series aired in 1953.

Helmed by producer Robert Maxwell, who was known for his hard-hitting film noir style of filmmaking, production took place at the RKO-Pathe' studios in Culver City, California in July of 1951. Budgeted at $400,000, and sponsored by Kellogg's and initially airing on ABC, it was soon sold to individual stations on a syndicated basis.

The other new cast members were reliable Bob Shayne as "Inspector Henderson," veteran actor John Hamilton as "Perry White," nineteen year-old Jack Larson as "Jimmy Olsen," and Phyllis Coates as "Lois Lane." Incredibly, all had worked under contract for Warner Brothers Studios at one time in their respective careers – as did Noel Neill.

Curiously, although there has been much speculation to the contrary, Phyllis Coates and Noel Neill have never met. They did appear in one film together, the cold war chiller *Invasion USA* (1951) but did not have any scenes together. There is absolutely no evidence whatsoever that would prove any type of meeting between the two "Lois Lanes" has ever taken place. At least one internet website has authored a fictional account between the two and at least one other went as far as to blatantly state that Noel had it written into her *Superman* contracts that she would have no contact with Phyllis. This writer can attest that he

George Reeves as Brent Tarleton in *Gone With The Wind*, 1939

THE ADVENTURES OF SUPERMAN: THE TELEVISION YEARS

has read all of Noel's *Superman* contracts and there is no inclusion whatsoever regarding restricting contact with other players. Any suggestion otherwise is pure fabrication.

With the release of *Superman and The Mole Men* in 1951, it too became an instant success. However, National Comics, for reasons that are still unclear, chose not to release the television scrics until February of 1953, in Los Angeles. Apparently, neither National nor Kellogg's was too pleased with the final production results. Hoping to attract an evening time slot, Bob Maxwell's finished product resembled the serials of old, with quick and brutal violence, shootings, deaths, and general mayhem. Although well-acted, produced and directed, these episodes were essentially filmed for an adult audience. The crew was one of the best around for such an action genre – many core members being part of the crew that filmed *Citizen Kane* – but National wanted to go in another direction.

After the first airing of the initial 26 episodes, National Comics quickly ordered up 26 additional episodes, but with a new producer and a new leading lady.

Whitney Ellsworth was hired to take over for the departing Bob Maxwell. A New Yorker with National Comics, "Whit" was no stranger to the *Superman* enterprise, having overseen the production of the superb *Superman Cartoon* series by the Fleischer Brothers in Miami, and the *Batman* serials of 1949. Well-liked as a scriptwriter, cartoonist, editor and producer, he fit the bill perfectly, and he rode the series successfully all the way to the end of the 1957 episodes. Whit understood that both National and Kellogg's sought a softer, lighter approach for the adventures of "The Man Of Steel," and that focus would directly lead to the marketing of the program toward children, Kellogg's target audience. Gone were multiple deaths by shootings, dark lighting, and overly grim-faced mobsters. "Superman" was

THE ADVENTURES OF SUPERMAN: THE TELEVISION YEARS

now less an angry, no-nonsense crime-fighter; but more of a self-reflective, much more humorous and engaging friend of the common man. In fact, all the roles became less serious and tended to lean more toward the humorous and absurd. "Perry White" would actually smile and laugh occasionally and the mobsters more closely resembled harmless, bumbling idiots; not quite the "Three Stooges," but close. It has been argued that the original (1951) episodes are more daring and creative; the writing more crisp with clearly defined purpose. Perhaps, but it is also a good bet the series might never had continued beyond the first year if the approach to production had not changed. It probably would not have maintained the interest of 10 year-olds, and would today be but a faint memory to all but a faithful few.

Phyllis Coates was signed for only the first 26 episodes. She was a terrific actress with lungs that could scream with the best of them. Phyllis' "Lois" was always suspicious of "Clark Kent," never deferring to him. She was portrayed as a self-assured, almost negative, character who knew who she was, what she wanted, and how to get it. She rarely smiled. This characterization was fitting for the role as defined by Bob Maxwell. Unfortunately, between the end of the first year and before the filming of the second year, she had committed herself to filming a pilot for a new television series that was not picked up. That left the door open for the return of the popular Noel Neill.

In May of 1953, Whit Ellsworth picked up the telephone and made the call that probably saved the long-term future of *The Adventures of Superman*, and rekindled the world's love affair with the "First Lady of Metropolis" that continues to this day.

When Noel Neill was offered the role she originated, she listened attentively, yet quietly. When Whit finished his pitch, she paused briefly, then graciously accepted his offer. Obviously, an audition was neither expected nor implied. After all, Superman, Inc. was lucky to have her back, and Ellsworth knew it. A few days later Noel began reviewing the scripts and one thing was certain – the episodes would be filmed just like the serials. Noel must have believed she was coming full circle:

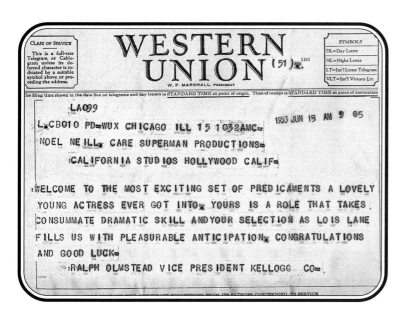

Arriving on the set at California Studios, 1953

THE ADVENTURES OF SUPERMAN: THE TELEVISION YEARS

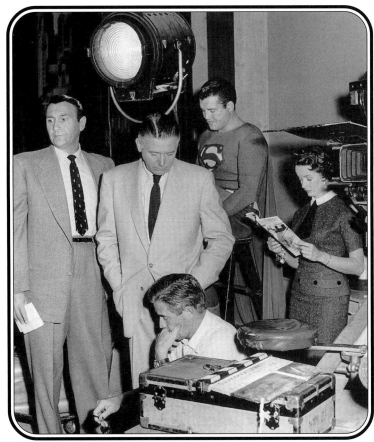

Going over their lines for *The Wedding of Superman*

"Again, there was no continuity in terms of following story lines or plots. We filmed all of the "Perry White" office scenes for all 26 episodes, one right after another; then all the scenes with all the heavies; then all the scenes in "Clark's" office or in my office, and so on. We had our call sheets which designated our lines and scenes, but little else. It was very hard to get into a character's frame of mind and still make it seem fresh and believable. But when I look at our shows today, I believe we pulled it off. We all worked hard, six days a week. Generally, I had to get up at 6:00 a.m. to make it to the studio by 8:00 a.m. First we had to go through makeup, then wardrobe. I had to fix my own hair because the producers were too cheap to hire a hairdresser. Nor did they outfit me with shoes or stockings; I had to bring my own from home. We normally worked until about 8:00 p.m., then you had twelve hours off until you were called back. Most of the time you could find one of us off in a corner somewhere going over our lines. We were so rushed that sometimes we didn't learn our lines until just before the scenes were to be filmed. It was so exhausting that by the time the week ended you pretty much collapsed until Monday morning. There really was no socializing after hours during filming because we just did not have any extra time to do any of that. What's funny, is that today, fifty years after we first worked together, I see Jack Larson far more now than I ever did when we were working on the show."

Although John Hamilton was an accomplished actor who appeared in many films, very little is known about his private life. Noel agrees that Hamilton was not an easy person to know.

"John was usually very quiet and often aloof. He was a wonderful actor who was always prepared and always professional. At the time I met him he was just a working actor trying to get through life. I know he had a young son who lived with him in his apartment on Hollywood and Vine. John had it arranged in his contract so that all of his residuals would go to his son upon his death. Unfortunately, it happened much sooner than any of us thought that it would. He died not long after filming the 1957

THE ADVENTURES OF SUPERMAN: THE TELEVISION YEARS

shows. One aspect of John that you don't really hear about was his marvelous sense of humor. On many occasions when Jack and I would burst into 'Perry White's' office and deliver our lines, John would come back with some naughty or risque remark, totally ruining the shot. Everyone always laughed because it was always so funny. It was so unlike anything that 'Perry White' would ever say. I've often thought that perhaps he did this because he couldn't remember his lines. However, once we re-set the shot, he always delivered like he was suppose to. On the other hand, we worked so hard that sometimes things got pretty tense, and when we got to that point, John would blurt out one of these unscripted lines. I think it just might have been his indirect way of telling everyone that we needed a break. Every once in awhile – just like everyone else –he would flub a line or miss a word or two here and there, but I think, for John, it was because of poor health or advancing age.

There were rumors years later that John had problems with alcohol and that he couldn't get his lines straight because of it. I have been asked if John would be less than sober on the set. Well, I was pretty aware of what went on back then, and I can tell you that I never saw or experienced anything like that with John and we worked together a lot. If he had problems with alcohol, he didn't bring it to the set. He was an old-time actor who prided himself on his professionalism. I do know that the show was easier to shoot when focused around 'Perry White's' desk, and John usually had his script on the desk right in front of him just in case he needed it, which was seldom. And when he did need to refer to his lines, he did so as if it was part of the script itself! That just shows what a good actor he really was. He knew all the tricks of the trade.

When there was talk of bringing the show back for 26 more episodes in 1959, John was to be replaced by Pierre Watkin, the original 'Perry White' from the *Superman* serials. Whit (Ellsworth) told me that the storyline would be that Perry's brother was going to take over as the editor of the *Daily Planet* while the 'Chief' was overseas working on a hot story."

Cast and Crew

77

THE ADVENTURES OF SUPERMAN: THE TELEVISION YEARS

None of the actors involved in the making of The Adventures Of Superman ever became wealthy from the series or from its repeated showings. Noel's first contract with Superman, Inc. in 1953 paid her the grand sum of $185 per episode. The most she ever made was on her 1957 contract, $225 per episode. She and Jack Larson shared the same agent and getting raises proved to be unrewarding experiences. Jack would later state that every time they got a raise, management would mope around and be angry with everyone for two weeks, before eventually getting back to normal. Residuals from the show apparently ended in 1965, which was the last year any of the actors received payments.

Interestingly, in Noel's 1953 contract it specifically states that she shall be paid the sum of $31.25 for "the sixth and all additional runs." Since 1953, Superman has never been off the air, running continuously all over the world, yet neither Jack nor Noel have been compensated for all of those showings since 1965.

Bob Shayne, the perpetually frustrated "Inspector Bill Henderson," who never solved a crime without "Superman's" help, truly was a fine actor, father, husband, and friend.

Noel found Bob to be a very competent actor and very easy to work with. But she knew him only on the set, never socializing after hours except on occasion of a rare end of season celebration or cast birthday party.

"Bob and I just did not run in the same circles. He had a wife and a family to raise and they did all the things that families typically do together. I was just married and, as always, spending a lot of time at the beach or traveling. So the only time I ever really saw him was on the set, and then not every week. But everyone did respect his work. The last time I saw Bob – and the last time we worked together – was in 1991 at the taping of a cable television program in Long Beach. It was good to see him and he seemed very happy and pleased to see both Jack and me."

Cast and Crew at Bob Shayne's Birthday Celebration

THE ADVENTURES OF SUPERMAN: THE TELEVISION YEARS

Bob Shayne stayed in acting long after the *Superman* era, taking parts in occasional films, and appearing in over 300 separate TV roles. He even wrote a script for the television series *Fantasy Island*, titled *Inspector Henderson Finally Gets His Man.* It would have been a wonderful return for the only man true Superman fans have ever known as Metropolis' chief of law enforcement. Unfortunately, the script apparently was never optioned by the producers.

Bob Shayne continued to offer solid acting performances up until the age of 90, with the role of "Reggie," the blind news vendor on the television series, *The Flash*. He died in 1992 at the age of 92 years.

In spite of all his film credits prior to his work in *Superman*, all his stage work after *Superman*, and his extensive and impressive accomplishments as a writer, producer, and director, Jack Larson will always be known as "Jimmy Olsen, cub reporter." "Golly" and "Jeepers" are the words most closely associated with this character and they were never delivered any better than when Jack Larson uttered them from 1951 to 1957. So closely identified is he to this role that more than fifty years later, hearing the distinct sound of his voice, and the cadence of his delivery, still immediately brings forth visions of "Jimmy Olsen." After years of attempting to escape the confines of this character, Jack Larson finally, and comfortably, found peace with the role he has long been identified with. In fact, rather than running

away from "Jimmy," he now embraces him. He recently filmed a much-publicized television commercial with Jerry Seinfeld for American Express; and he and Noel together filmed an episode of 1990's *Superboy* television series with Girard Christopher. In an August 2002 article by the *Associated Press*, which appeared in newspapers all over the world, Jack spoke of how fame really is not fleeting, especially if you are "Jimmy Olsen." The role gave him instant recognition, but it was always for being "Jimmy." And since his appearance has changed little over the years, he just decided to simply accept the fame of the role and have fun with it.

Noel has consistently and unfailingly voiced her admiration and respect for Jack Larson since the first day they worked together:

"Jack Larson is one of my closest and dearest friends. He is a brilliant man whose talent as a writer has renaissance-like quality. He can and has done so many things so well in TV, films, and the stage. When I think about his role as 'Jimmy,' I vividly recall an actor of great insight and charm, who thoroughly understood his role, and how to get the best from it. Occasionally he would lock horns with John Hamilton, who seemed to consider anyone under thirty as inexperienced. He

THE ADVENTURES OF SUPERMAN: THE TELEVISION YEARS

probably thought that Jack was brash because he was so confident and because he liked to call John by his first name. He expected to be addressed as 'Mr. Hamilton.' Jack certainly had a lot of energy and he displayed all of it on the show. I think most of our scenes together had us either in 'Perry White's' office getting yelled at, conspiring against 'Clark' for a scoop, or being tied together to a chair waiting to be blown up. Much of his dialogue was pretty silly, and Jack knew that. 'Whit' frowned on any actor changing their lines, so Jack did the best he could with what he had to work with. But he did it so well that most people now have that image of Jack as 'Jimmy' cemented in their memories."

In retrospect, Jack says that today that cross to bear is not that harsh. He has only a bowtie and sweater to contend with, while George Reeves had an entire costume to live down. Although his agent told him to just "take the money and run, Kid. No one will ever see this crap," Jack Larson has certainly proven that if one strives to put forth quality work, fame certainly is not fleeting; in fact, it can be long-lasting, positive, and well-deserved.

Jack Larson was the original voice of "Tony the Tiger" in television commercials in 1951. He and the other *Superman* cast members found extra work – and extra cash – doing cereal commercials for Kellogg's.

All cast members, that is, except Noel Neill.

For struggling and poorly paid television actors, TV commercials was where the real money was to be found. Shot quickly and in a day's time, an actor could easily double or triple what they were earning in a week in a series. Catering to an audience of young children who felt sway over their parents when it came to breakfast menus, Kellogg's learned early on that by using recognizable childhood heroes in their advertisements they could reap tremendous returns. For reasons not fully explained to Noel at the time, Kellogg's chose to exclude her from these lucrative deals. The original excuse given for not using her talents was that since this was a family show and most of the commercials revolved around the breakfast table, they thought it improper to show a single woman (Lois Lane) having breakfast with single men (Jimmy, Clark, Perry, and Bill). What is implied is that one or the other performed a "sleepover." If all the commercials had taken place at the breakfast table, then that explanation would have had merit. However, Kellogg's also aired several other commercials that did not focus around morning breakfast and of which Noel would have easily undertaken without controversy. But Kellogg's in the 1950s had a resoundingly wholesome image to maintain and the general consensus seems to be that they wanted to avoid any possibility of a scandal. They simply chose to travel the safe and conservative road – all the way to the bank.

Much of the success of The Adventures Of Superman can be tied directly to the believability of George Reeves as both "Clark Kent" and "Superman." The extent of his influence on the lives of millions

THE ADVENTURES OF SUPERMAN: THE TELEVISION YEARS

of viewers simply cannot be overstated. While *The Adventures Of Superman* is the most popular science fiction television series ever filmed, it is also one of the few series that has crossed several generations of viewers and maintained its popularity. Incredibly, the program shows no sign of slowing down. Cable networks TV Land and Nick At Nite both ran the series in the 1990s, and TV Land ran a *Superman Marathon* in October of 2002, that garnered its highest ratings in years.

George Reeves' portrayal of the "Man Of Steel" is without precedent in either television or film and his fame for this role has risen to a standard that can only be described as legendary. His popularity has spawned a reverence from a legion of admirers all across the planet. Thousands of fans have created internet websites in his honor; best-selling books have been written about his life; and literary newsletters and booklets have been created that serve to further the memory of George Reeves. But one of the grandest displays of honor is the Annual George Award presented each year to the person who best represents the ideals of George Reeves. This award ceremony takes place during the second weekend of June of every year at the annual Superman Festival in Metropolis, Illinois. This festival has been known to attract in excess of 30,000 visitors and the numbers have risen each year. Metropolis is also home to the world-famous Super Museum, with renown Superman collector Jim Hambrick as curator. Noel Neill has been welcomed as homecoming queen at this event, as she modestly gathers rousing standing ovations whenever she enters a room. Some have suggested that these ovations are not only meant for Noel, but for George, as well. Noel and Jack Larson are the last living direct links to George and the series, so this outstanding show of gratitude speaks volumes about the esteem with which they are held.

Although George Reeves and Noel Neill both were contract players for Paramount Pictures in the 1940s, they never appeared in any production together, and did not actually meet until June of 1953. Noel remembers the scene quite vividly:

THE ADVENTURES OF SUPERMAN: THE TELEVISION YEARS

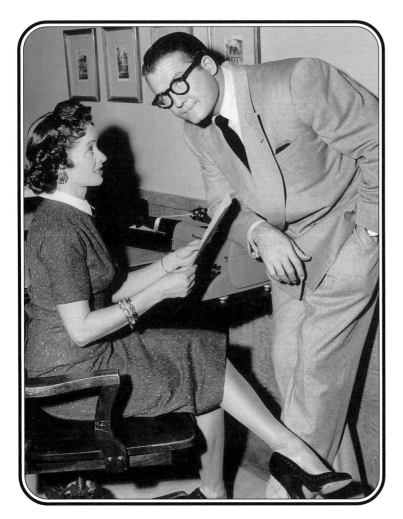

"I didn't meet George until our first scene together on the set of the filming of *Superman*. I walked up to him, introduced myself, and we exchanged pleasantries. He had that big, wide boyish grin. We got right down to business. But at one point early in the rehearsing stage, I remember that the director, Tommy Carr, just didn't like how I was saying the line, 'Gee, Superman, am I ever glad to see you!' He had me do that line over and over again. I repeated that line so many times that I began to get a little upset and started to shed a tear. George saw what was happening and immediately asked for a break. He walked over to Tommy and calmly said, 'Why don't you give the kid a break? It's hard to come into an already established family and do this just the way you want her to.' I was so grateful to George for sticking up for me. That is so uncommon in this business. The thing that really upset me was that I already knew how that line should be read, but Tommy just wouldn't let it go. But after George intervened, he eased up and let me do it my way – and I've been doing it my way ever since.

I also recall I was glad that George seemed so easy to work with, not like some others I had worked with in the past. He was just so easy-going. I learned later that he had the ability to memorize most of his lines in one reading, and that is not easy to do.

In many ways, George was just like John Hamilton. He, too, would say naughty things in lieu of the actual script and break everyone up – while the producers were screaming 'the money, the money, we're wasting film!' John and George sometimes exchanged 'blue' humor amongst themselves whenever I wasn't around to hear it. George was a true 'southern gentleman' and southern gentlemen didn't talk like that in front of young ladies!"

THE ADVENTURES OF SUPERMAN: THE TELEVISION YEARS

Superman, Inc. published a press release in 1951 that stated that George Reeves had bested over 200 other individuals for the part of "Superman." Noel believes that this was typical, standard propaganda that studios were long capable of submitting to a gullible public.

"I really don't think George got the job purely on talent alone, although he was more than qualified, and most likely the best qualified. I knew he had taken up with Toni Mannix, the wife of MGM boss, Eddie Mannix, some years prior to *Superman*. I also knew that she had promised to make him a star if he would divorce his wife, which he did. I liked Toni, but it was no mystery to me that she wielded a lot of clout around town; and if she thought George should have had the part, then it wouldn't have surprised me if she had helped land it for him. Toni and I did get along very well. She was fun being with, but I didn't spend an awful lot of time with her. She trusted me with George; so for Toni, that's really what mattered most. I do remember going over to the house she and Eddie owned and lived in. One day I sat in the kitchen drinking a cup of coffee when Eddie walked in wearing a bathrobe. He was so nice to me, so pleasant. I liked him very much. Then George waltzed in and exchanged a few brief, but pleasant words with Eddie, and off he went with Toni. They were like a family of three, all very happy and comfortable with this arrangement."

The camaraderie that the entire cast enjoyed was uncommon. Perhaps some of this was due to the unbelievable true fact that most of the cast, prior to their acting careers, sought careers in journalism. Noel wrote for *Women's Wear Daily*; Jack was editor of the *Montebello High School Oiler*; and Bob Shayne was a real estate reporter for the *Illinois Daily Pad*. From the serials, Kirk Alyn had enrolled in journalism school at Columbia University, and Pierre Watkin was the actual editor of the *Sioux City*

THE ADVENTURES OF SUPERMAN: THE TELEVISION YEARS

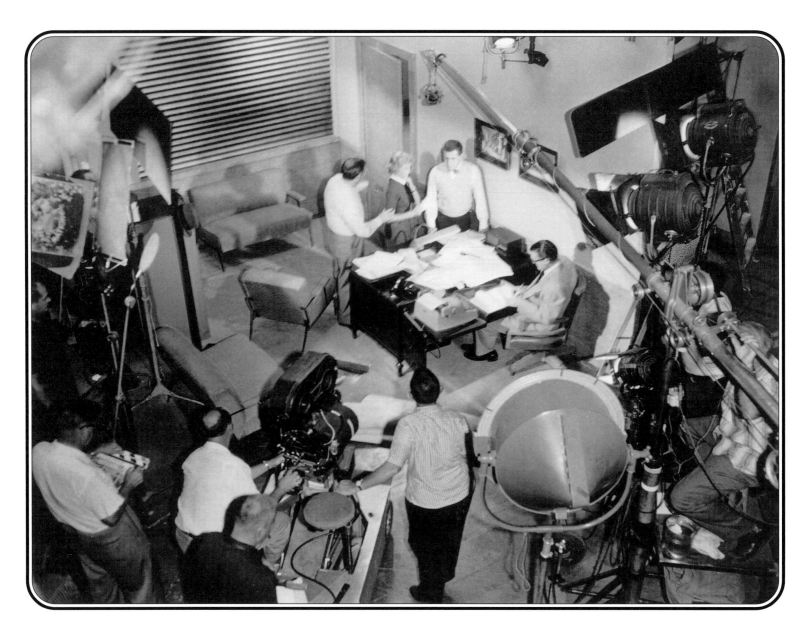

Tribune. Although he had writing aspirations, it is not known if George actually published any of his works. So having more than an inkling of how the newspaper business operated could not have been anything but a positive reinforcement for this talented cast. Further, and as the tie that binds, every single cast member was a seasoned live stage performer long before the television series. Each person had extensive experience in both dramas and musicals, and each had impressive film acting careers.

Putting the cast's acting careers in perspective, the silly, mundane lines they had to speak each week must have seemed unchallenging to them, yet they still delivered them like the tight, collective, well-oiled machine that they were. They truly considered themselves a family, and as such they knew instinctively how to work with one another to get the best from each part. As time passed, and episode after episode was completed, that family unit became tighter and more protective of one another. Noel offhandedly noted that most of the time, especially during the 1956 and 1957 seasons, they were so accustomed to the same sets, the same dialogue, similar story lines, and working with a lot of the same actors, that having use of a director was almost an incidental act.

"We had performed so many of the same scenes and same words with the same actors, that we knew how to hit our mark and move on. Often, we joked that we could have done without a director, although

THE ADVENTURES OF SUPERMAN: THE TELEVISION YEARS

both Tommy Carr and George Blair were excellent directors. It is just that there was not a lot of variety in terms of creative sets or unusual location shots where a great director would have been indispensable."

Noel also seems to casually cast-off the notion that George Reeves was a highly skilled director, judging from his directorial debut on *Superman*, as so many other authors of Reeves' books have suggested.

"If I hadn't already known that George had directed the last three episodes of the last season, I wouldn't have noticed the difference. Again, we were so good at working together as a cast, that all George had to do was just have us say a line faster or slower, louder or softer, which is how I understand George Lucas directs. This is not to say that George was not a great director; it is just that after the first two seasons, the series typically did not give any director too many opportunities to show their greatness, and George was no exception."

But more than anything, Noel was impressed with George Reeves the actor.

"George really was a great and wonderful actor. I knew it, we all knew it, and I hope George saw what we saw. If you look back at his work in the episode, *The Face & The Voice*, George actually plays four different and distinctly separate characters: one as 'Clark Kent,' then "Clark' as 'Superman;' the mobster 'Boulder' who looks like 'Superman,' and then 'Boulder' as 'Superman.' Acting in that episode would have been very confusing for a lessor actor, but George jumped into these parts with ease. But to also consider that he played dual characters in every episode for six years is almost beyond comprehension. In spite of his great body of work on *Superman*, I don't think we ever got to see the true depth of his talent. I think George's best work was still ahead of him. I do know that sometimes he thought the role

THE ADVENTURES OF SUPERMAN: THE TELEVISION YEARS

THE ADVENTURES OF SUPERMAN: THE TELEVISION YEARS

of 'Superman' was demeaning or beneath his abilities. After appearing in so many good films in great roles, it must have seemed like a step down for him at the time. I only wish George could have lived long enough to know the joy that he has given to so many people for so many years."

In 1974, Whitney Ellsworth penned a handwritten letter to the editor of the *Los Angeles Times* in response to a previously published article on Noel Neill. In part, he wrote:

"As producer of most of the episodes (of the TV series) it was my pleasure and good fortune to sign Miss Neill to the role to which she brought a quality of broad appeal for viewers of all ages both here and abroad. In the 25 years that *Superman* has been continuously on the air, she has almost certainly been seen more often by more people than any other leading lady of stage, screen, or television, with the possible – just possible – exception of Lucy."

Just what is it about Noel Neill's unshakable performance as "Lois Lane" through 30 chapters of the serials and 78 episodes of the television series, that has endeared her to us? How do we objectively measure the impact of her influence on a world of viewers without falling victim to the shameless use of maudlin terms and phrases? We do so through studying the dynamics of her relationship with her *Daily Planet* counterparts and by examining those areas specific to Noel's interpretation of the role of "Lois Lane."

The "quality of broad appeal" that Ellsworth writes of most certainly entails these areas of interpretation: the drive to succeed; the use of humor; emotional range; and physical attractiveness. If we dismiss Noel's earlier claim that she did not really play "Lois Lane," she simply played herself, one can begin to understand the roots of this broad appeal. While Noel Neill does possess some of the same personal qualities of "Lois Lane," that alone would not begin to explain our appeal for her "Lois." Ultimately, she has to play "make believe" and that is where the difference lies. Any number of actresses probably could have played the role convincingly, but it is HOW Noel played the part that has left the lasting impression.

"Lois Lane" of the comic books is a true go-getter. Her drive to succeed is second to no man when it comes to scooping "Clark Kent" for a great story. Noel takes this approach to a different level by injecting humor and a smile where a grimace or sneer would have made us think she was mean or impersonal. In more than one sequence, "Lois" tells "Clark" that he can use her car, then tosses him the keys to her Nash with the flat tire. As she happily drives away in the company car, laughing at his predicament, poor "Clark" is left standing with his hands in his pockets. We have to laugh as well, because we know that it will not be the last time "Lois" thinks she has one over on "Clark." We also know that it is only a matter of inconvenience to him and that "Lois" will get her comeuppance in the end. But it all ends in good humor because "Lois" is kept guessing and part of the game for the viewer is knowing what "Lois" does not ever seem to figure out – who "Superman" really is.

THE ADVENTURES OF SUPERMAN: THE TELEVISION YEARS

THE ADVENTURES OF SUPERMAN: THE TELEVISION YEARS

Clearly not a one-dimensional character, and not unlike most people in real life, Noel's "Lois" is vulnerable, both physically and emotionally. The display of her range of emotions is both subtle and wide-ranging and offers us the talent of Noel in all her glory. Unfortunately, she was not given too many moments to showcase her considerable acting range, but when she did get center stage, she took enthusiastic advantage of these few opportunities. Three of her favorite television episodes, *The Tomb Of Zaharan*, *The Wedding Of Superman*, and *Panic In The Sky*, also happen to be the same three for which she is often praised for her work.

THE ADVENTURES OF SUPERMAN: THE TELEVISION YEARS

The Tomb of Zaharan is a story of supposed mistaken identity. "Lois" is thought to be the reincarnated Queen of Zaharan, 5,000 years old. She and "Jimmy" are kidnapped and transported to Zaharan to be entombed in the Queen's final resting place. Dressed in scant period clothing, for the first time viewers got to see far more of Noel Neill than anyone ever imagined was possible on a 1950's family-oriented program. While she was always easy to look at, what was only hinted at in her tight-fitting business suit suddenly became a reality to long-suffering 10 year-old boys (and no doubt, their fathers). Rather than playing it straight as a tragic drama, she played it for laughs, coupled with just the right hint of believable emotional quandary, to make this a timeless celluloid gem.

In the acclaimed *Panic In The Sky*, the second most expensive *Superman* episode ever filmed (after *The Unknown People, aka The Mole Men*) "Superman" loses his memory after purposely colliding with a fast-approaching asteroid that threatens Earth. The quiet, yet highly dramatic opening sequence of Lois' almost crying pleas to understand what was happening, sets the somber tone and mood for the remainder of the episode. She never seems more vulnerable than at this moment. You sense the

THE ADVENTURES OF SUPERMAN: THE TELEVISION YEARS

Scene from *Panic In The Sky*

THE ADVENTURES OF SUPERMAN: THE TELEVISION YEARS

The Wedding of Superman

Why is Noel laughing? George forgot his belt!
The Wedding of Superman

helplessness that she feels and you want to help her, yet you cannot, and for once, neither can "Superman." This very short sequence conveys both the warmth of the character and her emotional isolation and quiet desperation.

Finally Noel was never better than in *The Wedding Of Superman*. In this episode "Superman" proposes to "Lois" and they are to be married. Again, the episode commences not in the usual fashion. We find a close-up of "Lois" and she says, "I'm Lois Lane, and this is my story." This is Noel's own special time in the light, and in accordance with such, she is given three separate outfits to wear. Noel actually seems to glow in the softness of the camera lens as she goes from being angry toward the gangsters who try to ruin her wedding, to the love and tenderness she expresses to "Superman." This is also, incidently, George Reeves' most tender moment in the entire series. Her most dramatic scene comes at the end when she movingly sheds tears at the sudden realization that what she thought was very real, was only a dream.

The tears that Noel shed for this scene were very real. But as dramatic as this scene is, it is not the initial shot that was kept. The scene was filmed twice. After the first shot, the entire cast and crew gave Noel a very loud round of applause. George, Jack, and even John Hamilton all said that they thought that she had done a wonderful job. However, the sound man then noticed that there were problems with the audio, so they had to shoot this difficult moment all over again! Noel was not too sure that she could summon the same emotions needed to convey what she was feeling the first time; but with George's encouragement she not only replicated the first shot, but probably improved upon it.

THE ADVENTURES OF SUPERMAN: THE TELEVISION YEARS

This dynamic second effort and purposely conveyed emotional vulnerability and warmth pervaded virtually all the episodes in which Noel appeared. Although Noel's "Lois" is also funny and fun, she is still deadly serious about her job as a reporter and her drive to succeed. She never lets us forget that she is frequently kidnapped by mobsters, insulted by "Perry White," and occasionally belittled verbally by "Clark Kent," yet she still gets the job done. In fact, more than a few early viewers from the television series, who are now adults, have written to Noel over the years and thanked her for being such a positive female role model. Many have become actual newspaper reporters themselves because of her inspiring portrayal. Some have even thanked her publicly in their columns. Bob Greene of the *Chicago Tribune* once wrote that Noel Neill was the first working woman many of us saw on television. "Lois Lane" was her own woman who had her own apartment, made her own way in life, and depended on no one (except "Superman") to survive life's trials and tribulations – which happens to also describe Noel Neill. ★

The Wedding of Superman

THE ADVENTURES OF SUPERMAN: THE TELEVISION YEARS

Chapter 6:
How Long Has It Been Since You've Sung – Sober?

HOW LONG HAS IT BEEN SINCE YOU'VE SUNG – SOBER?

After the production of *The Adventures of Superman* ended in 1957, Noel received a telephone call from George. She was a little surprised to hear from him, because George rarely called anyone.

"Hi, Noel," he said in his usual friendly, upbeat voice. "How long has it been since you've sung – sober?"

Noel answered with a laugh. He then told her of his plan to form a song and dance group that would travel across the country performing at state and county fairs. He said he knew she was a great performer, and would she consider taking the stage with him? She liked what she was hearing, so she readily agreed to take part in this enterprise. Noel had never been one to think too hard or too long about a proposal. It either appealed to her, or it didn't, and she liked to stay with her original decision. Considering her long-term track record for success, everything told her that she was making the right decision by trusting her instincts.

A few days later, Noel arrived at George's home on Benedict Canyon Road to rehearse. George decided that he would sing and play stand-up bass. His childhood friend and fellow actor, Natividad Vacio, would play guitar and bass, along with his friends Hon Hollington on accordion and Freddie Hernandez also on guitar. Gene LaBell, who worked on the show doing stunts, was signed to play "Mr. Kryptonite" in a skit wrestling with George. After several days of rehearsal on George's back patio (the home itself being too small), all agreed that they were ready to tour. Interestingly, there seem to be several conflicting accounts of Toni Mannix being part of this group, but Noel says that this just was not so.

"Toni and George were a very discreet couple. On the set, she would bring George his lunch and stay in his dressing room, not making herself too visible. She did not attend any of our rehearsals nor did she travel with us on the tour. After all, she was married to a major studio boss, so she had to be very careful where she was seen. Eddie Mannix had his own girlfriend, so he was just as discreet."

August 17, 1957, Albuquerque, New Mexico

HOW LONG HAS IT BEEN SINCE YOU'VE SUNG – SOBER?

August 20, 1957, Pueblo, Colorado

Noel borrowed a few outfits from MGM Studios, courtesy of Toni Mannix. One of those outfits would later be known as the "Stanwyck dress," named for Barbara Stanwyck who wore the exact same silvery outfit in the film *Lady of Burlesque*, of which Noel also had a part as an impressive tap-dancing chorus girl. Although the tour has often been described as a highly organized, smartly marketed, and well-attended operation, Noel offers a radically different perspective.

"The 1957 Fair Tour was financed entirely by George. When we left from Los Angeles we really had no bookings other than the first site, the Colorado State Fair in Pueblo. George's agent, Art Weissman, put a couple of large ads in the local newspaper, *The Pueblo Chieftain*, just prior to our arrival. It was incredibly hot – well over 100 degrees. We did three shows over the course of three days, all in the hot, open-air sun. All were well-attended and well-received. It was such a great beginning to what we thought would be a wonderful run. We traveled from site to site in two cars, with George, Art & Nati in one car, and myself and the others in the second car. We didn't stay at four-star hotels – after all, this was George's money – but the rooms were nice and comfortable. This tour started on such a high note, but it didn't last very long. After Pueblo, George was not at all happy. When not on stage performing, he pretty much stayed by himself in his room and drank. This routine occurred at each city we visited. George told me that he was very upset that Art had not done more to promote the tour. He was expecting extensive radio, television, and newspaper coverage at each site, but apparently very little of that was

HOW LONG HAS IT BEEN SINCE YOU'VE SUNG – SOBER?

done. It was disheartening to come into a town and then leave without doing more than one or two media interviews, or pose for any publicity shots. It seemed the more we toured, the more depressed George became. The low point came at a show in North Carolina. Everyone was embarrassed and humiliated to learn that only 3 people were in attendance – a young boy and his parents – who sat right in the middle of the front row. Well, as they say, 'the show must go on' and it did; we gave a great show to just those three individuals. It was a very sobering experience. Later that night, for George, it was a very intoxicating experience."

It had been at least a decade since Noel had performed on a stage before a live audience. A self-described "ham" she found she had not lost any of her old tap-dance moves and her singing voice was in fine shape. She truly loves to perform, and having done so since a child, she has no fear of the stage whatsoever. Although some of the attendance was very low, the group did find satisfaction in the quality of their performances, and George, like Noel, seemed his happiest on stage.

Although the Fair Tour was scheduled to continue for several more weeks, the group decided to disband after the September 13th show at the Reading Fair in Reading, Pennsylvania. They were well-received in Reading, but George had already lost thousands of dollars on the tour, and he was losing more every day they were on the road. At the completion of the Reading show everyone packed up and

HOW LONG HAS IT BEEN SINCE YOU'VE SUNG – SOBER?

drove back to Los Angeles, save for George and Art, who headed to Columbus, Ohio for an appearance for the Columbus Safety Campaign.

Several days after George arrived back in Los Angeles, he received a telephone call from Noel. She explained that she had thought the whole matter through and decided that she would like him to keep her fee. She knew that the tour was a financial disaster, so she did not want to make things any worse for him. He argued with her for a few minutes, but eventually ceded to her persuasion. He knew that what she was doing was the honorable thing to do, and he stated his appreciation for her understanding of this difficult situation.

Noel would not see George again until the funeral of John Hamilton, more than a year later. ★

HOW LONG HAS IT BEEN SINCE YOU'VE SUNG – SOBER?

HOW LONG HAS IT BEEN SINCE YOU'VE SUNG – SOBER?

August 26, 1957, Asheville, North Carolina

HOW LONG HAS IT BEEN SINCE YOU'VE SUNG – SOBER?

August 26, 1957, Asheville, North Carolina

Chapter 7:
Gee, Superman, Are We Ever Glad To See You!

GEE, SUPERMAN, ARE WE EVER GLAD TO SEE YOU!

Contrary to his screen image, John Hamilton was actually a very quiet and very private individual. For someone who had acted in more than two hundred films dating back to 1932s *A Window In Piccadilly*, he did not seem to have had very many close friends in the film industry. Thus it should have come as no surprise that there were few mourners at his funeral following his fatal heart attack on October 15, 1958.

The remaining cast members from *The Adventures Of Superman*, including George Reeves, arrived to pay their respects to their old colleague. For such a somber occasion, George seemed unusually chipper and in fine spirits. He spoke to Noel of his new pending projects, and to her, he appeared happy and full of life.

Eight months later, Whitney Ellsworth called Noel at her home and told her that National Comics had given the green light for twenty-six new episodes, and that the scripts had just arrived from New York. He asked her to come by the studio to see if her old suit still fit.

It was on June 14, 1959 that Noel arrived at ZIV Studio on Santa Monica Boulevard and found both George and director George Blair sitting at a card table enjoying a game of gin rummy. Again, George was in a very upbeat mood. He gushed about directing half of these new episodes and having less screen time so that he could focus more on the production side of the show. He talked of touring Australia and having the inside track to directing several non-Superman film projects. Clearly, to Noel, many good things were on the horizon for George Reeves.

However, two days later, on June 16, 1959, the world awoke to the shocking news of the death of "Superman." The official coroner's report concluded that George had died by his own hand using a .30 caliber German Luger, although many unanswered questions remained. The best detailed account of that fateful night can be found in Jan Henderson's book, *Speeding Bullet*. Many of George's fans and friends now believe that he was either murdered, or was a victim of a lover's quarrel. Both Jack Larson and Noel Neill do believe one thing for certain; barring any sudden revelations, we will probably never truly know what really happened to George Reeves.

Following George's funeral, Jack was approached by the show's producers to star in his own series as the very popular "Jimmy Olsen." George would continue to appear as "Clark Kent" and "Superman" using stock footage. Jack was appalled by this seemingly insensitive and macabre proposal. He made it very clear that he wanted nothing to do with anything that would trade on his friendship with his old friend.

Another proposal by the producers included bringing back Noel, Jack, and Bob Shayne in their respective roles, inserting Pierre Watkin as "Perry White" (which was already expected after John Hamilton's death), and recasting the roles of "Clark Kent/Superman" with another actor. But National Comics firmly and decidedly cancelled this proposal. George Reeves was so well-identified with these characters that National was unwilling to risk ridicule and likely failure by replacing a person who was already beginning to be perceived as a legend. So coveted was this perception that it was almost twenty years later that National Comics (later DC Comics) finally gave the go-ahead for the feature film with the new "Superman," Christopher Reeve.

Throughout her entire career, Noel Neill has always been regarded by her peers as an actor's actor: always on time, always prepared, and she always knew her lines. But after the death of George, her interest and enthusiasm for the profession waned, partly from the devastation she felt after losing her friend and partly from suddenly being "typed" as "Lois Lane." She seriously, but briefly, considered

GEE, SUPERMAN, ARE WE EVER GLAD TO SEE YOU!

LaVere, David and Noel Neill, 1960

Noel at Santa Monica Beach, 1960

Santa Monica Beach, 1956

doing commercials, but abandoned that idea when it seemed casting directors could not see her as anything but the "girl reporter" for *The Daily Planet.*

So in 1960, at forty years of age, Noel Neill suddenly retired from show business. Although she never made a lot of money from the television show, she still managed to save what she earned, and she bought a home in Santa Monica Canyon. It is that very same home that she continues to live in today, more than forty years later.

Much of the 1960s were quiet, reflective times for Noel. She began to travel extensively – something she had always enjoyed with her mother – and she finally achieved a lifelong dream: she became a self-described "beach bum." As a member of the Santa Monica Swim Club, Noel developed a seemingly permanent and deep, rich tan, and she continued to fully indulge in her favorite sport, beach volleyball. But toward the end of the decade, boredom had set in, and although she was comfortable financially, she chose to go back to work – but not back to show business.

GEE, SUPERMAN, ARE WE EVER GLAD TO SEE YOU!

Santa Monica Swim Club

Noel, 1967

Brown's Temporary Service, located on Wilshire Boulevard, was a company specializing in temporary secretarial services. Through a friend, Noel applied as a "temp" and was accepted. Who would have thought that only ten years removed from "Lois Lane and Superman," Noel Neill would once again be banging the keys, but this time for real? Noel became a "Brownie" and she was happy in her work. She had no lofty preconceptions about the job, nor did she believe that her social standing had changed after a lifetime under the lights. She simply wanted to go back to work and this was work she enjoyed and did well.

One of Noel's first jobs at Brown's sent her to work for the Milton J. Wershow Company, an auctioneering and real estate firm on La Brea Avenue in Los Angeles. She was so well-liked that she was optioned from Brown's as a full-time employee, eventually staying almost eight full years.

Soon thereafter, Noel found herself back at a major film studio doing similar work for United Artists. Situated in the Irving Thalberg Building at MGM Studios, she started in the publicity department, but quickly worked her way into the television division, helping to sell television programs to individual stations west of the Mississippi.

GEE, SUPERMAN, ARE WE EVER GLAD TO SEE YOU!

But in January of 1974, Noel received a telephone call from a student at Monmouth College in New Jersey, that once again brought new challenges and new opportunities – and another career.

"I started my day as I normally did, with a cup of coffee and a plain donut. I drove over to United Artists, sat down, and began opening the morning mail when my telephone rang. The fellow on the other end said his name was 'Jeff' and that he was a student at Monmouth College. I thought it was just another telephone call until he asked for me specifically. When I identified myself, he said the words that will stay with me for the rest of my days: 'Miss Neill, would you please consider coming to Monmouth College and talk to our students about your career as Lois Lane?' I was absolutely floored. I didn't know what to say. No one had ever asked me to speak before a group of college students, so I wasn't too sure what to expect. We agreed on a date and a fee of $800. This was far more money than I had ever made doing *Superman*, and here they wanted me for only an hour. I just didn't know what to think. From all the years of filming *Superman*, I did not receive a single piece of fan mail. I just figured I wasn't too popular. I learned years later – in the 1980s – that I was receiving sacks of mail regularly, but the show's producers had it all sent to New York to be processed and answered. I never saw any of it. But based entirely on this false assumption, I couldn't imagine why anyone would be interested in seeing me, much less listen to anything I had to say.

Well, there's an old saying in show business that goes, 'if you're not sure of your act, then give them something to clap to and sing along with. They'll leave happy, but they won't know why.' So I borrowed a 16mm copy of the episode, *The Tomb of Zaharan*, which the college paid an exhibit fee to show. I

GEE, SUPERMAN, ARE WE EVER GLAD TO SEE YOU!

wanted to recreate as much of the "Lois Lane" aura as I could, so I contacted Whit Ellsworth to learn what had happened to my old suit. Whit had a lot of things in his garage, but the suit was not one of them. I then drove over to Western Costumes, the show's outfitters, but the suit could not be located there, either. To this day, that old suit refuses to turn up. I didn't want to just show up in a plain outfit, so a friend made me a suit similar to the one I wore on the show, and I purchased a pillbox hat similar to the one I wore in the second Superman serial. My hair was much shorter at the time, so I found a red wig that I thought came close to how I had styled my hair back then.

The day of the event finally arrived. It was April 9, 1974, and I was nervous and unsure of myself. Jeff had initially told me that they expected not more than two-hundred people, at best. But when he picked me up at the hotel to drive me over to the campus, it was then that I learned that over a thousand students were waiting for me! This reception was totally unexpected and unbelievable. The film was run first and every time I was in a scene – which was most of the episode – the kids would just whoop and holler. Finally, the film ended, and the room was completely dark. Someone handed me a microphone, and in my best 'Lois Lane' voice I shouted, 'Gee, Superman, are we ever glad to see you!' The lights went up and I walked out onto the stage and the place just erupted in booming applause, with the longest standing ovation I had ever witnessed. I was so overwhelmed by the moment that I began to cry. But the more I cried the more they applauded, so I knew I had to stop doing that. After several minutes everything calmed down and I grabbed the mic and began to talk about my years as "Lois." When I finished some twenty minutes later there was another standing ovation, followed by a lengthy question and answer period. After that, I spent about an hour signing autographs. Those Monmouth kids were simply the best. That experience was one of the true highlights of my life."

Between 1974 to 1978, Noel Neill would go on to address the students of more than fifty colleges and universities nationwide. Incredibly, just about every setting was the same; overflow crowds and standing ovations wherever she appeared. After Monmouth, she added a humorous piece to her presentation which offered a lighthearted approach to the episodes, and to show how hard acting really

GEE, SUPERMAN, ARE WE EVER GLAD TO SEE YOU!

was. She brought along her script from *Panic In The Sky* and pulled students out of the crowd to play the various characters in the episode. As expected, those amateur actors tripped and fumbled over their words to the delight and glee of the audience. Years later, some of those very same students still write to Noel and say that the highlight of THEIR college years was acting on the same stage with the "original Lois Lane."

Sometimes the individuals in these groups were not always as well-mannered as perhaps they were raised to be. Owing to the times of free-flowing speech and the infancy of political radicalism on campus, students would occasionally pose questions to Noel that might better have been left unspoken, such as the young man who asked if she and George ever engaged in a relationship that was more than platonic ("No"). Or the young bearded fellow who commented that, as a child, he would run home from school and slide himself under the television set so that he could look under Lois' dress. In spite of such inappropriate encounters, Noel took it all in the light that it was given. Commenting on such behavior in an interview with the *Washington Post,* Noel put such humorous incidents exactly where they belonged:

"Bless their little hearts. They'll say anything that comes into their little heads." ★

GEE, SUPERMAN, ARE WE EVER GLAD TO SEE YOU!

Chapter 8:
Noel Neill Today

NOEL NEILL TODAY

As much as Noel Neill loved traveling the college lecture circuit, by the end of the 1970s and approaching the age of sixty, the grind of the road was beginning to take its toll. Although still in superb physical condition, she found it increasingly cumbersome to juggle her duties at United Artists and still find the time to fully conduct these shows. The bosses at United Artists were very agreeable to her requests for time off, because each time she visited a new city the local newspapers would publish a brief description of her work at United Artists. But Noel felt that the numerous days out of the office effected her ability to perform at the high level that she expected of herself. So she made the conscious and deliberate decision to not take any additional college speaking engagements after 1978.

However, that decision that did not apply toward other work. In 1977, Noel received a telephone call from the producers of the new feature film, *Superman*, starring the unknown actor Christopher Reeve. They were in production on location in Southern Alberta, Canada. They asked if she would consider making an appearance in the film as Lois Lane's mother. Both executive producer Ilya Salkind and director Richard Donner were fans of the serials and the television show, and through Noel's appearance, they wanted to acknowledge the work of all the actors and crew members who had come before them. Noel did not ponder this decision, but immediately accepted their offer and began packing her bags for a week's stay in Canada. In the meantime, she received another telephone call. It was a representative for Kirk Alyn. *Variety* had reported the news of Noel Neill being added to the cast and this person was literally demanding that Noel talk Salkind into hiring Kirk as well. After a few minutes of listening to this virtual tirade, Noel simply hung up on her mid-sentence. She thought that would be the end of it until she boarded the plane for Alberta the next day and there seated in the row next to her was Kirk Alyn. Somehow, Kirk was added to the cast as the father of "Lois Lane." Noel never asked how he got the part and Kirk never volunteered that information to Noel.

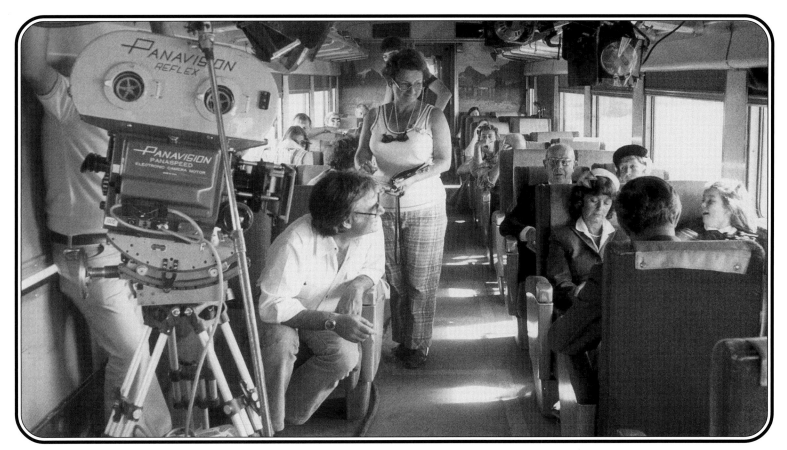

On the set of 1978's *Superman*

NOEL NEILL TODAY

Superman Location, Barons, Southern Alberta, Canada
From left: Executive Producer Ilya Salkind, Noel Neill, Cathy Painter as young Lois Lane,
Kirk Alyn, and *Superman* Producer Pierre Spengler

NOEL NEILL TODAY

Noel with Christopher Reeve, 1994

By appearing in 1978's *Superman*, Noel became the only actress ever to play in all three forms of *Superman* cinema (the serials, the television program, and now the feature film) and each with a different "Man Of Steel."

With her work on *Superman* completed, Noel returned to California and her job at United Artists. She continued to work exceedingly well in the television department until 1981, at which time she and the twenty-five other employees in the Los Angeles office were terminated. United Artists had bankrolled Michael Cimino's hugely expensive film *Heaven's Gate*. The failure of this film almost single-handedly bankrupted this once-fine studio. Undaunted, as actors are used to doing, Noel applied for unemployment, and briefly looked for other work.

Less than a week after leaving United Artists, Noel heard from an old friend, Terry Kingsley Smith, a Hollywood writer of many years. He told her of a young television actor who was in need of someone to help coordinate the processing of his fan mail. While filming his show in Hawaii, the mail was beginning to pile up in Los Angeles. Being a conscientious person, he was not comfortable with all this correspondence going unread, unopened, or unprocessed. So Noel took on a new role in professional life as the coordinator of fan mail for Tom Selleck, star of *Magnum, P.I.* Today, more than twenty years later, she remains in this capacity on a mostly part-time basis. She and Tom Selleck also remain good friends. Noel describes him as a hard-working, considerate, and exceptionally loyal person who prides

NOEL NEILL TODAY

Noel with a very young Tom Cruise, February 17, 1982, New York

himself not only on the quality of his work, but on the quality of his relationships. She believes that the longevity of his career has been long-rooted in these practiced values.

Much of the 1980s and 1990s consisted of a series of personal appearances as the keeper of the flame for *The Adventures Of Superman.* These appearances, along with friend Jack Larson, included participation in film festivals, television programs honoring the 50th Anniversary of *Superman*, the annual Superman Festival in Metropolis, Illinois, and documentaries on the life of George Reeves. Not quite retired from acting, both Noel and Jack also received great reviews for their work in an episode of 1992's *Superboy* with Girard Christopher.

During the same two decades, Noel continued to travel extensively. Her personal journeys found her trekking in Tibet, climbing the Great Wall of China, entering the Great Pyramid of Giza, and cruising the waterways of Alaska. Her wanderlust never satisfied, she continues to plan even greater adventures.

NOEL NEILL TODAY

Noel with Jack Larson and Girard Christopher, 1991, *Superboy*

The next few years could easily find her at the Taj Mahal, or navigating the Amazon in her search for new experiences.

Entry into the twenty-first century – and Noel's eighth decade of life – did not mean a lessening of Noel's always busy schedule. In fact, this decade may yet prove to be her busiest since her Paramount days. Again, she and Jack were teamed together by being honored in 2001 by the City of Los Angeles for their incomparable and time-honored work in *The Adventures Of Superman*. In 2002, TV Land, which began the decade by broadcasting all 104 episodes of the series, conducted a massive nationwide media promotion of the best episodes of the series, utilizing the best ambassadors of the program, Noel and Jack. Their participation resulted in the most positive reaction from viewers in years.

NOEL NEILL TODAY

Today, Noel Neill continues to actively speak at conferences and film festivals about her life in film, and she lovingly considers Metropolis, Illinois her true second home. ★

NOEL NEILL TODAY

Noel with Jack Larson, Burbank, California, 2002

Truth, Justice, & The American Way
The Life And Times Of Noel Neill
The Original Lois Lane

~ Epilogue ~

It is amazing to see your life through the eyes of a biography. As I read through these pages little snips of incidences kept popping up. It was like looking at life through the wrong end of a telescope. The descriptions and pictures of times long ago brought back wonderful remembrances of friends and dancing partners lost but to my memories. It was wonderful to read about my childhood, my many travels with "Tiny," and to once again make acquaintance with those who would touch my life in various ways. For me, these were such happy, happy thoughts to be cherished, and many long-forgotten times to be revisited. I think of the small, personal moments I shared with those who are a part of my life, and it brings a private smile to my face. It is not unlike a movie where the focus is a "trip back through time." But that is what a biography is for, isn't it? I hope you have enjoyed it with me.

Noel Neill
March 2003

Noel Neill and Larry Thomas Ward
April 25, 2002

Truth, Justice, & The American Way
The Life And Times Of Noel Neill
The Original Lois Lane

RECOMMENDED READING

Alyn, Kirk. **A Job For Superman.**
Hollywood, CA: Kirk Alyn, 1971.

Barbour, Alan, G. **Days Of Thrills & Adventure.**
London: The MacMillan Company, 1970.

Bifulco, Michael. **Superman On Television.**
Grand Rapids, Michigan: Michael Bifulco, 1998.

Grossman, Gary. **Superman: Serial To Cereal.**
New York: Popular Library, 1976.

Hart, John. **Cowboys In The Kitchen.**
Avon, New York, 2000. bigmick45@webtv.net

Hayde, Michael J. "The Life & Death Of George Reeves."
Remember Magazine, February/March, 1995.

Henderson, Jan Alan. **Speeding Bullet: The Life & Bizarre Death Of George Reeves.**
Grand Rapids, Michigan: Michael Bifulco, 1999.

Lowther, George. **The Adventures Of Superman.**
Bedford, MA: Applewood Books, 1942, 1995.

Moore, Clayton. **I Was That Masked Man.**
Dallas, Texas: Taylor Publishing Company, 1996.

Truth, Justice, & The American Way
The Life And Times Of Noel Neill
The Original Lois Lane

APPENDIX I:
Dance School Credits From Age 4 Years To Age 17 Years.

1925
"The Sick Doll"
Performed Lead Role
Seton Guild Dramatic Recital
Norway Hall, Minneapolis, MN

1926
February 8
"The Joys of Traveling"
"7-Act Vaudeville"
Group Singing & Dancing
Seton Guild Dance Arts Dept.
Jefferson Junior High School, Minneapolis, MN

March 16
"Milady's Boudoir"
Performed Role of "Powderpuff"
& Performed "Ballet & Novelty Dances"
Seton Guild Dance Arts Department
Jefferson Junior High School, Minneapolis, MN

June 5
"Piano Pupils In Recital"
Performed "Little Granddaughter"
Irene McCaffrey Presents
Seton Little Theatre, Minneapolis, MN

1928
May 22
"Spring Recital"
Solo Spanish Dance
Played the Role of "Pierrette"
in the Musical: "Pierrette We All Adore You."
Seton Guild At Jefferson Jr. High School
Minneapolis, MN

October 28
"Children's Play Hour"
Read "The Punishment Of Mary Louise"
WDGY Radio, Minneapolis, MN

1928 continued
"Static"
Incarnation Players Dramatic
Club of the Incarnation
Group Singing Role & "Dance Duet"
with Randolph Norris
Minneapolis, MN

1929
November 27
"Piano Recital"
Noel Neill as "Reader"
Fardahl Conservatory Of Music
Leamington Hotel, Minneapolis, MN

December 18
"Washington Evening School Christmas Party"
Performed "Tap Dance"
Minneapolis, MN

December 20
"Zuhrah's Ladies Society Annual Yule Social"
Performed "Character Dances"
Zarthan Hall - Masonic Temple

1930
January 18 & 19
"Rip Van Winkle"
Performed group singing
Juvenile Repertory Company
Minneapolis, MN

February 22
"Washington Birthday Party"
Performed "Spanish Dance"
& Role of "Teddy Bear"
The Minneapolis Elks Club
Seton Guild Dance Arts Dept., Minneapolis, MN

February 27
"Quality Street"
Performed "Singing & Dancing"
Juvenile Repertory Company
Minneapolis, MN

APPENDIX I

1930 continued
May 20
"Dancers Will Tango"
Performed Tango With Randy Norris
Seton Guild Dance Arts Dept.
Jefferson Jr. High School, Minneapolis, MN

1931
January 16
"Rockford High School Athletic Program"
Performed "Character Dances"
with Randy Norris
Benefit Program
Rockford, MN

November 20
"Junior Novelty Program"
Group Role as Dancer
MacPhail School, Minneapolis, MN

1932
March 9
"Last Welfare Benefit Entertainment"
Parents & Teachers' Association
Scholarship Fund
Performed "Character Dances"
Jordan Jr. High School
Knickerbocker School of Dancing
Minneapolis, MN

June 4
"Dance Recital"
Minneapolis College of Music Auditorium
Performed a "Slave Dance," "Cymbal Dance,"
"Rumba," and "Hand Drill"
Billert & Sullivan Dance Studio
Minneapolis, MN

June 10
"Annual Junior Banjo Musical & Recital"
Performed "Cymbal Dance," played tenor Banjo on "Cheerful Tidings," "Blue Of The Night,"
& "Telltales"
Presented by Gould Studios
Emerson School, Minneapolis, MN

June 22
"Toymaker's Dream"
Performed "Rumba Rhythm"
Laura Hoffoss Dance Studio
Minneapolis Auditorium, Minneapolis, MN

1932 continued
December 15
"How Christmas Was Saved"
Performed "Dancing Doll"
Bryant Auditorium, Minneapolis, MN

1933
January 20
"My Spanish Sweetheart"
Performed Role of "Carmen,"
a Spanish Dancer Operetta
Bryant Junior High School, Minneapolis, MN

May 16
"Annual Recital"
Performed "Cuban Dance Numbers"
Jefferson Junior High School, Minneapolis, MN

June 2
"YWCA Dance Recital"
Performed "Character Dances"
Billert & Sullivan Dance School, St. Paul, MN

June 9
"Annual Junior Recital
Performed two songs on banjo:
"Rock-A-Bye Moon" & "Lil-Liza Jane"
Gould Banjo, Mandolin & Guitar Studios
Emerson School, Minneapolis, MN

June 15
"Minneapolis Teacher's League"
Performed "Character Dances"
Caserta School of the Dance
Joppa Lodge Hall, Minneapolis, MN

December 14
"Christmas Throughout The Ages"
Performed "Dutch Girl," "Spanish Dancer,"
& "Doll Dance"
Bryant Junior High School, Minneapolis, MN

1934
April 20
"Purple Towers"
Operetta
Performed Role of "Dancer"
The Girl's Glee Club
Bryant Junior High School, Minneapolis, MN

APPENDIX I

1934 continued
June 1
"Vaudeville Night"
Performed "Classical Waltz"
with Jerry Ravine
Bryant Junior High School, Minneapolis, MN

November 22
"Autumn Frolic"
Performed a "High Kick, a Specialty Dance"
West Evening High School, Minneapolis, MN

1936
March 13
"Comedy Concert"
Vaudeville Show
Performed "Spanish Dance"
Central High School, Minneapolis, MN

1937
April 8 & 9
"Vaudeville Show"
Performed as "Featured Vocalist"
Central High School, Minneapolis, MN

DANCE STUDIOS

1925
"Seton Guild of Dance & Dramatic Arts"
Genevieve Ward, Instructor of Dancing
Vera McNiff, Director of Drama

1930
Knickerbocker Dancing School

1932
Billert & Sullivan Dance Studios
Mildred Billert & Kathleen Sullivan

1933
Gould Banjo, Mandolin, & Guitar Studios
C.W. Gould (Mr.)

1933
Laura Hoffoss Dance Studio

1934
Caserta School of Dance

Truth, Justice, & The American Way
The Life And Times Of Noel Neill
The Original Lois Lane

APPENDIX II:
Professional Performance Credits
From Age 10 Years To Age 17 Years

1930
December 20-27
"Kid Nite Follies"
("Miniature Musical Comedy")
"RKO Supreme Vaudeville with Pat Henning, Sidney Tracey & Bessie Hay, The Liazeed Demnati Troupe & Comedians Nelson Clifford & Marie Marion"
Movie: "She's My Weakness" with Sue Clark & Arthur Lake
RKO Orpheum Theatre, Minneapolis, MN

1931
April 22
"Donaldson's Afternoon Wedding"
Fashion Show & Entertainment
Performed as a Page
Donaldson's Dept. Store, Minneapolis, MN

April 23
"RKO Orpheum Knickerbocker Review"
Performed as Model: "…will present new fashions for the younger set."
RKO Orpheum Theatre, Minneapolis, MN

June 15
"Knickerbocker Kiddie Revue"
With Vaudeville Acts: Larry Rich & His Oomphas; Phil Rich; Edler & Reed Brothers; Marion Sunshine, The Peanut Vendor
Movie: "Everything's Rosie," with Robert Woolsey
RKO Orpheum Theatre, Minneapolis, MN

December 12
"RKO Kiddie Revue On The Stage"
Performed "Spanish & Specialty Dancing"
With Vaudeville Acts: The Woodard Sisters; Jerry Ravine; Billy Stonebreaker; Noel Neill
Lincoln Theatre, Monticello, MN

1931 continued
December 20-27
"Snow White & The Seven Dwarfs"
The Bainbridge Players
Performed role of "Ursula"
Shubert Theatre, Minneapolis, MN

1932
January 8 & 9, 1932
"RKO Kiddie Review"
Vaudeville acts: Woodard Sisters; Jerry Ravine; Noel Neill; and Billy Stonebreaker
Movie: "Near The Trail's End" with Bob Steele
Palace Theatre Hector, Minneapolis, MN

February 19 & 20
"Kiddie Revue - Five Pecks of Pep"
Movie: "Wild Horse" with Hoot Gibson
Also Chapter 7 of: "The Galloping Ghost" with Red Grange
Oriel Theatre, Minneapolis, MN

February 27
"The Oriole Kiddie Revue"
Movie: "Charlie Chan's Chance," "Fiddling Around," "The Hatchet Man"
The Auditorium, Red Wing, MN

March 18 & 19
"Gillis Grafstrom"
"Three-Time Olympic Figure-Skating Champion"
Performed as a member of "The Figure Skating Club - The Children Foursome"
Minneapolis Arena, Minneapolis, MN

March 20
"Mrs. Wiggs Of The Cabbage Patch"
The Bainbridge Players
Performed Role of "Lena Krausmier" and "Dolores Woodard & Noel Neill Offer a Dance"
Shubert Theatre, Minneapolis, MN

APPENDIX II

1932 continued

April 1
"Informal Models Will Display
New Types Of Coiffures"
Informal Opening Of Beauty Salon
Performed as Model
Powers Department Store, Minneapolis, MN

April 12
"See The Kiddie Revue"
Card Party & Entertainment, Rosary Society
Sacred Heart Auditorium, Minneapolis, MN

May 1
"The Orioles"
Noel Neill, Jerry Ravine, The Woodards,
& Billy Stonebreaker
Empress Theatre, Minneapolis, MN

May 28 & 29
"The Oriole Kiddie Revue"
"Comedy, Spanish & Tap Dancing"
Noel Neill, Jerry Ravine, The Woodards,
& Billy Stonebreaker
The Princess Theatre, Minneapolis, MN

July 17
"The Orioles"
Movie: "Amateur Daddy" and "In Walked Charlie"
Mounds Theatre, Minneapolis, MN

July 22 & 23
"Kiddie Revue - The Orioles"
With Vaudeville Act: Mickey McGuire Comedy.
Movie: "Heart of New York" with George Sidney
Chapter 8 - "Battling With Buffalo Bill"
The Garden Theatre, Minneapolis, MN

August
"Showboat Motif"
Zonta Club Dinner Program
Performed a "Dance Number"
Leamington Hotel, St. Paul, MN

September 13 & 14
"Kiddie Revue & Style Show"
Sears, Roebuck & Co., Minneapolis, MN

1932 continued

September
"Sears 46th Anniversary Follies"
Performed song and dance numbers
Sears, Roebuck & Co., Minneapolis, MN

September 24
"Kiddie Revue"
Ladies Night Party
The Elks Club, Minneapolis, MN

October 8
"Donaldson's Children's Program"
Billert & Sullivan Dance Studio
Performed "Songs & Tap Dancing"
Donald's Dept. Store, Minneapolis, MN

October 21
"Play Night"
Performed "Spanish Dance"
YWCA, St. Paul, MN

October 22
"Kiddie Show"
Performed "Songs & Dance"
Donaldson's Dept. Store, Minneapolis, MN

October 27
"Kiddie Revue & Style Show"
"Clever Child Stars"
Performed "Songs & Dance"
Donaldson's Dept. Store, Minneapolis, MN

October 28
"Big Show For Kiddies"
Performed "Dance Numbers"
Donaldson's Little Theatre, Minneapolis, MN

November 1
"Dinner Club of Minneapolis"
Dancing by Vincente Escudero
Performed "Dancing Exhibition"
At The Women's Club, Minneapolis, MN

December 3
"Children's Musical Program"
Performed "Songs & Dance"
Donaldson's Little Theatre, Minneapolis, MN

APPENDIX II

1932 continued

December 16
"Toyland Revue"
Performed "Songs & Dance"
Sears, Roebuck & Co., Minneapolis, MN

December 18
"The Magic Mill"
The Bainbridge Players
Performed Role of "Dancing"
Shubert Theatre, Minneapolis, MN

1933

January 28
"Kiddie Revue"
Performed "Songs & Dance"
The Colonial Room, Leamington Hotel
Minneapolis, MN

February 11 & 12
"Billert & Sullivan Kiddie Revue"
Performed "Cymbal Dance" & "Spanish Dance"
American Legion, St. Cloud Jr. High School
St. Cloud, MN

March 24
"Ward's Spring Fashion Revue"
Performed as Fashion Model
Montgomery Ward & Co., St. Paul, MN

April 6
"Kiddie Revue & Style Show"
Easter Headline Days
Performed "Songs & Dance," and modeled clothing
Sears, Roebuck, & Co., Minneapolis, MN

May 24
"Parade Of The New"
Modeled New Fashions
Curtis Hotel, Minneapolis, MN

June 2
"The Graduation Frolic"
Sang and danced individually, and with The Woodard Sisters
Golden Valley Golf Club, Minneapolis, MN

1933 continued

August 6
"Internationally Famous Kiddie Revue"
Mound 29ers Day Celebration
Performed "Songs & Dance"
Municipal Park, Lake Minnetonka, MN

September 6 & 7
"Kiddie Style & Dance Show"
Performed "Songs & Dance"
Sears, Roebuck, & Co., Minneapolis, MN

1934

February 14
"St. Valentine's Day Cabaret"
Performed "Spanish Dance" with Jerry Ravine
Temple Israel, Minneapolis, MN

March 30
"Jerry & Ginger" (as Ginger O'Neill)
Performed "Songs & Dance"
The Oaks, Minneapolis, MN

June 18
"Jerry & Ginger"
"Dancing A Little Bit Different"
Old Heidelberg Inn, Superior, Wisconsin

June 19
"Jerry & Ginger"
Performed "Songs & Dance"
The Oaks, Minneapolis, MN

July 1
"Jerry & Ginger"
Movie: "The Lost Patrol" with Boris Karloff
Radio Theatre, Minneapolis, MN

August 5
"Jerry & Ginger"
"Internationally Famous Troupers"
Sixth Annual 29ers Day Celebration
Performed "Songs & Dance"
Municipal Park, Mound, Lake Minnetonka, MN

October 20
"Formal Fall Closing Party"
Performed several dance numbers
Golden Valley Golf Club, Minneapolis, MN

APPENDIX II

1934 continued
December 8
"Ravine & O'Neill"
"Stage Show"
Movie: "Dr. Monica" with Kay Francis
Lyceum Theatre, St. Paul, MN

December 8
"Jerry Ravine - Ginger O'Neill"
With Skip Burke's Revelers
Performed "Songs & Dance"
Fasbender's Fawn Room, St. Paul, MN

"During the Summer of 1934"
Minnesota State Fair
Wisconsin State Fair
Iowa State Fair
Tri-State Fair
Performed both individually and with
The Woodard Trio

1935
January 10
"Miller's Jewels Revue" & "Miller's Jewels of 1935"
Minneapolis Banquet
Minnesota Federation Of County Fairs
Minneapolis, MN

March 8
"WCCO Barn Dance"
Radio Broadcast
"Three Musical Woodards"
The Grand Theatre, Minneapolis, MN

April 27
"The Woodard Trio"
Minikahda Club, Minneapolis, MN

May 4 & 5
"The Three Musical Woodards"
"The Syncopated Vaudeville Revue"
Move: "The Silver Streak"
Lyceum Theatre, St. Paul, MN

June 12
"The Woodard Trio"
14th Annual Northwest Radio and Home
Appliance Show
Minneapolis, MN

1935 continued
June 15
"The Three Woodards"
"Dolly, Marles & Ginger"
"Professional Vaudeville"
Movie: "Forsaking All Others" with Joan
Crawford and Clark Gable
Beacon Theatre, Minneapolis, MN

August 16
"The Woodard Trio"
County Fair, Fond Du Lac, WI

Labor Day
"Ginger O'Neill" & " The Woodard Trio"
Tavern on the Green, Waterloo, Iowa

1936
February 14
"Noel Neill - Miss Variety"
Blue Rubbon Nite Club, Albuquerque, NM

April 18
"Jimmie Pidgeon's Orchestra
Featuring Noel Neill"
Phi Epsilon Alpha's April Frolic
Glenwood Chalet, Minneapolis, MN

May 9
"Ginger O'Neill" & "The Woodard Trio"
12th Annual Banquet
Minnesota Power & Light
Spalding Hotel Ballroom, Minneapolis, MN

May 28
"The Woodard Trio" also "Ginger O'Neill"
Sixth Annual Banquet Of The Minneapolis
Jr. Association Of Commerce
Nicollet Hotel, Minneapolis, MN

June 20
"The Three Woodards"
Big Time Vaudeville
Lyceum Theatre, St. Paul, MN

June 25 & 26
"Miller's Jewels of 1936" & "The Woodard Trio"
Rolla Celebration, Munro Theatre, Rolla, ND

APPENDIX II

1936 continued
July 1
"The Woodard Trio"
VFW Convention, Detroit Lakes, MN

September 28
"The Woodard Trio"
The Flame Room, Hibbing, MN

October 16
"The Woodard Trio"
Elk's Lodge, Minneapolis, MN

December 17
"Noel Neill with Leonard Keller & His Orchestra"
KSTP Radio
Advertising Club of Minneapolis, MN
Curtis Hotel, Minneapolis, MN

December 21
"Eddie Rames & His Music With Miss Noel Neill"
The Country Club, Minneapolis, MN

December 30
"The Woodard Trio"
WTCN Radio
Hotel Lowry, St. Paul, MN

1937
February 9
"Noel Neill - Queen of Market Week"
Twin Cities Market Week
Minneapolis, MN

February 21
"Ginger - This & That In Music"
The Roxy Theatre
Minneapolis, MN

June 24-26
"Ginger"
Specialty Dancer with Miller's Jewels of 1937
Benson Fair Celebration
Minnewauken, ND

Truth, Justice, & The American Way
The Life And Times Of Noel Neill
The Original Lois Lane

APPENDIX III:
Noel Neill Singing Performances After 1937

(not listed in Film or Television Credits)

1938
May
"El Chancellor Band"
Vocalist
Hotel Del Mar, Del Mar, California

June-July-August
"Del-Mar Turf Club"
Vocalist
Del Mar, California

Fall
"Omar's Dome"
Vocalist
Los Angeles, California

Fall
"Somerset House"
Vocalist
Los Angeles, California

1939
March
"Jimmy Walsh & His Orchestra
Featuring Noel Neill"
Mark Hopkins Hotel
San Francisco, California

April - September
"Del Mar Turf Club"
Vocalist
Del Mar, California

1940
February
"Ray Merrill & His Aristocrats
With Noel Neill As Chanteuse"
Cafe Lamaze
Sunset Strip, Beverly Hills, California

April
"Ray Merrill & His Orchestra
Featuring Noel Neill"
Santa Rita Hotel
Tucson, Arizona

1957
August - September
"On Tour With George Reeves"
1957 Fair Tour

Truth, Justice, & The American Way
The Life And Times Of Noel Neill
The Original Lois Lane

APPENDIX IV:
Noel Neill Films From 1941 To 2002

"Henry Aldrich For President" — 1941
"Miss Polly" — 1941
"Henry And Dizzy" — 1942
"Cavalcade Of Travel" — 1942
"Miss Annie Rooney" — 1942
"Lady Of Burlesque" — 1943
"Henry Rocks The Cradle" — 1943

Paramount Contract - March 1943

"Let's Face It" — 1943
"You Can't Ration Love" — 1943
"Prairie Chickens" — 1943
"Salute For Three" — 1943
"Standing Room Only" — 1944
"Fun Time" — 1944
    (Paramount Short)
"Henry Aldrich's Little Secret" — 1944
"Red, Hot, & Blue" — 1944
"The Road To Utopia" — 1944
"Our Hearts Were Young & Gay" — 1944
"Rainbow Island" — 1944
"Out Of This World" — 1944
"And The Angels Sing" — 1944
"Caribbean Romance" — 1944
    (Paramount Short)
"Here Come The Waves" — 1944
"Are These Our Parents?" — 1944
    (Monogram)
"The Hour Before Dawn" — 1944
"Duffy's Tavern" — 1945
"You Hit The Spot" — 1945
    (Paramount Short)

"Hold That Blonde" — 1945
"College Queen" — 1945
    (Paramount Short)
"Masquerade In Mexico" — 1945
"The Stork Club" — 1945
"Bring On The Girls" — 1945
"Junior Prom" — 1945
    (Monogram Teenagers Series)
"High School Scandals" — 1945
    (Monogram Teenagers Series)
"To Each His Own" — 1945
"Freddie Steps Out" — 1946
    (Monogram Teenagers Series)
"High School Hero" — 1946
    (Monogram Teenagers Series)
"Blue Skies" — 1946
"Old Gray Mayor" — 1946
    (Monogram Teenagers Series)
"Monsieur Beaucaire" — 1946
"The Well-Groomed Bride" — 1946
"Over The Santa Fe Trail" — 1947
"Smash-Up, The Story Of A Woman" — 1947
"The Fabulous Joe" — 1947
"Brick Bradford" — 1947
    (Columbia Serial)
"Sarge Goes To College" — 1947
    (Monogram Teenagers Series)
"Vacation Days" — 1947
    (Monogram Teenagers Series)
"Smart Politics" — 1948
    (Monogram Teenagers Series)
"Adventures Of Frank & Jesse James" — 1948
    (Columbia Serial)

APPENDIX IV

"Superman" 1948
    (Columbia Serial with Kirk Alyn)

"Gun Runner" 1948

"Man Or Mouse" 1948

"Music Man" 1948

"Campus Sleuth" 1948
    (Monogram Teenagers Series)

"Glamour Girl" 1948
    (Columbia)

"When My Baby Smiles At Me" 1948
    (Fox)

"Beyond Glory" 1948

"Blue Gardener" 1948

"The Big Clock" 1948

"Are You With It" 1948

"Born To Sell" 1948

"Manhattan Folksong" 1948

"Cactus Cut-Ups" 1949
    (RKO)

"Son Of A Badman" 1949

"Forgotten Women" 1949

"Sky Dragon" 1949

"Osage" 1949

"The James Brothers of Missouri" 1949

"Atom Man Vs. Superman" 1950
    (Columbia Serial With Kirk Alyn)

"An American In Paris" 1951

"Submarine Command" 1951

"Whistling Hills" 1951

"Ghost Riders" 1951

"Gentlemen Prefer Blondes" 1952

"The Greatest Show On Earth" 1952

"Marshall's Reward" 1952

"Montana Incident" 1952

"Invasion USA" 1952

"The Lawless Rider" 1954

"Siege At Red River" 1954

"Superman's Peril" 1954

"Superman In Scotland Yard" 1954

"Superman In Exile" 1954

"Superman Flies Again" 1954

"Superman & The Jungle Devil" 1954

"Stamp Day For Superman" 1954

"Superman" 1973

"Superman" 1978

"In A Single Bound" 2000

"7th Annual Asheville Film Festival" 2002

Truth, Justice, & The American Way
The Life And Times Of Noel Neill
The Original Lois Lane

APPENDIX V:
Noel Neill Radio And Television Appearances From 1943 To 2002

1943
"Variety Show"
  WGXYZ Channel 4 Hollywood
  One-Half Hour of Vaudeville
  MC, Singer, Dancer, and Model

1950
"The Cisco Kid"
  (Episode: "Chain Lightning")

"Racket Squad"
  (Episode: "The Long Shot")

1951
"The Lone Ranger"
  (Episode: "Letter Of The Law")

"The Seven Graces"
  Fireside Theatre

1953-1957
"The Adventures Of Superman"
  (Role: Lois Lane)

1954
"The Ray Bolger Show"

"Public Defender"
  May 20, 1954

1974
"The Mike Douglas Show"
  December 24

"Town Talk"
  WKYT-TV
  September 24
  Lexington, Kentucky

"A Talk With Lois Lane"
  WLEX-TV
  September 24
  Lexington, Kentucky

1975
"Lois Lane & The Batmobile"
  Channel 44 "Variety"
  November 7
  St. Petersburg, Florida

1976
"Day By Day"
  WVCM-TV, Channel 19
  Delta College
  January 29

"Regis Philbin's Saturday Night
  In St. Louis"
  KMOX-TV, Channel 4
  St. Louis, Missouri
  February 1

"NBC Weekend"
  Superman Documentary
  February 7

"Superman: The Birth, Legend and Nostalgia"
  KCOP-13
  Los Angeles, California
  September 8

"The Tomorrow Show With Tom Snyder"
  NBC Television
  New York, New York
  October 25

1977
"Good Morning America"
  CBS Television
  New York, New York
  October 28

1978
"Morning Radio"
  KRLA - Hit Radio 11
  Pasadena, California
  September 20

APPENDIX V

1986
"The Jim Eason Show"
  KGO-FM
  San Francisco, California
  August 30

"The Frank Dill & Mike Cleary Show"
  KNBR - 68 FM
  San Francisco, California
  August 30

"Labor Day Superman Marathon"
  KICU-TV 36
  San Jose, California
  August 31

1987
"Where Are Lois & Jimmy Now"
  KCOP - TV 13 News
  Los Angeles, California
  November 12

1988
"CBS This Morning"
  New York, New York
  February 29

"Entertainment Tonight"
  Superman's 50th Anniversary
  Los Angeles, California
  February 29

"Superman's 50th Anniversary"
  A Celebration Of The Man Of Steel
  CBS Television
  New York, New York
  February 29

"Morning Exchange"
  Superman Exposition Show
  Cleveland, Ohio
  June 17

"1988 Superman Expo Parade"
  WVIZ-TV
  Cleveland, Ohio
  June 17

1988 continued
"Live On Five"
  WEWS-TV
  Cleveland, Ohio
  June 17

1989
"A Current Affair"
  Who Killed Superman?
  May 17

"Entertainment Tonight"
  The George Reeves Mystery
  May 17

1990
"Entertainment Tonight"
  Lois Lane & Superman
  February 5

"KCNX - Action News"
  On The Queen Mary
  Long Beach, California
  October 31

1992
"Talk Of The Town"
  Studio 3
  Long Beach, California
  October 31

1993
"Sci-Fi Buzz"
  Superman In Hollywood Features
  Part I
  December 3

1994
"Sci-Fi Buzz"
  Superman In Hollywood Features
  Part II
  February 24

1996
"CBS This Morning"
  New York, New York
  March 29

APPENDIX V

1996 continued

"America After Hours"
  CNBC
  New York, New York
  April 11

"RE-TV Awards Night"
  Channel 11 News
  New York, New York
  September 11

"A Current Affair"
  The Death Of George Reeves
  May 17

2000

"A&E Biography: George Reeves:
  Perils Of A Superhero"
  February 16

2001

"The Early Show With Bryant Gumbel"
  CBS Television
  New York, New York
  January 31

"Los Angeles County Televised Board
  Of Supervisors Meeting"
  Mayor Antonovich Superman
  Presentation
  Los Angeles, California
  July 10

2002

"TV Road Trip"
  The Travel Channel
  Metropolis, Illinois
  April 7

"Jack Larson, Noel Neill, &
  Candy Clark On Route 66"
  KNBC - Channel 4
  Burbank, California
  August 30

"BBC Television News"
  Route 66 Rendezvous
  London, England
  August 30

2002 continued

"KTTV - Channel 11 News"
  Fox Network
  Los Angeles, California
  August 30

"KCOP - 13 News"
  UPN Television
  Los Angeles, California
  August 30

"Karen Grant Show"
  KRSK - AM
  Monterey, California
  September 19

"KOSZ Radio"
  Salt Lake City, Utah
  October 1

"Newstalk With Paul W. Smith"
  WJR Radio
  Detroit, Michigan
  October 2

"Giovanni & Kim"
  WPRO Radio
  Providence, Rhode Island
  October 2

"Johnny & Murphy"
  KQRC Radio
  Kansas City, Missouri
  October 2

"Newstalk With Tom Hughes"
  WGST Radio
  Atlanta, Georgia
  October 2

"Mark & Pam"
  WMUS Radio
  Grand Rapids, Michigan
  October 2

"Extra"
  Nationally Syndicated TV News
  MTV Studios
  Santa Monica, California
  October 3

APPENDIX V

2002 continued

"Newstalk With Jim Scott"
  WLW Radio
  Cincinnati, Ohio
  October 3

"Rocky & Blaine"
  WDVD Radio
  Detroit, Michigan
  October 3

"Mike Bennet Show"
  WHUD - Radio
  New York, New York
  October 3

"Tim & Karen"
  KLOU Radio
  St. Louis, Missouri
  October 3

"Dave & Teresa"
  ABC Radio
  Pure Gold - National Oldies
  Syndicated to over 150 Markets
  Nationwide
  October 3

"KABC Radio"
  Los Angeles, California
  October 3

"WROK Radio"
  Rockford, Illinois
  October 3

"Inside Edition"
  Superman 50th Anniversary
  MTV Studios
  Santa Monica, California
  October 3

"Fox News Network"
  Superman 50th Anniversary
  MTV Studios
  Santa Monica, California
  October 3

Truth, Justice, & The American Way
The Life And Times Of Noel Neill
The Original Lois Lane

APPENDIX VI:
1957 Fair Tour With George Reeves

August 20-22	Colorado State Fair Pueblo, Colorado
August 26-27	City Auditorium Asheville, North Carolina
August 28	Memorial Auditorium Raleigh, North Carolina
August 30-31	Township Auditorium Columbia, South Carolina
August 31	City Auditorium Charlotte, North Carolina
September 9-11	Kentucky State Fair Louisville, Kentucky
September 13	The Reading Fair Reading, Pennsylvania

Truth, Justice, & The American Way
The Life And Times Of Noel Neill
The Original Lois Lane

APPENDIX VII:
Noel Neill College Lectures From 1974 To 1978

1974

April 9
Monmouth College
West Long Branch, New Jersey

April 17
College Of The Holy Cross
Worcester, Massachusetts

April 18
Suffolk University
Boston, Massachusetts

April 18
Emerson College
Boston, Massachusetts

April 20
Massachusetts Residential Program
Boston, Massachusetts

May 22
Superior State College
Sault Ste. Marie, Michigan

June 20
Grand Valley State College
Allendale, Michigan

September 9
Nassau Community College
Garden City, New York

September 24
University of Kentucky
Lexington, Kentucky

October 10
State University College
Brockport, New York

1974 continued

October 12
New York State University
Geneseo, New York

October 18
LaSalle University
Philadelphia, Pennsylvania

November 2
Upsula College
East Orange, New Jersey

November 3
Shippensburg University
Shippensburg, Pennsylvania

November 4
E. Stroudsburg State College
E. Stroudsburg, Pennsylvania

November 5
Kutztown University
Kutztown, Pennsylvania

November 6
Montgomery Community College
Blue Bell, Pennsylvania

November 7
West Chester State College
West Chester, Pennsylvania

November 19
University of New York
Fredonia, New York

November 20
Alfred University
Alfred, New York

APPENDIX VII

1975

January 18
Tufts University
Boston, Massachusetts

January 20
State University College
Geneseo, New York

January 23
University of Buffalo
Buffalo, New York

February 7
George Washington University
New York, New York

February 8
American University
Washington, D.C.

February 17
University of Virginia
Charlottesville, Virginia

February 18
University of North Carolina
Chapel Hill, North Carolina

February 19
University of Kansas
Lawrence, Kansas

February 27
Northeastern University
Boston, Massachusetts

March 9
Slippery Rock University
Slippery Rock, Pennsylvania

March 11
University of Wisconsin
Milwaukee, Wisconsin

March 13
University of Madison
Madison, Wisconsin

1975 continued

April 9
University of Hartford
Hartford, Connecticut

April 10
Queens College
Queens, New York

April 14
University of Richmond
Richmond, Virginia

September 14
University of Illinois
Chicago, Illinois

September 20
The College of Lake County
Grayslake, Illinois

September 27
University of Oklahoma
Tulsa, Oklahoma

October 7
Normandale Community College
Bloomington, Minnesota

October 11
University of Southern California
Los Angeles, California

November 20 & 21
Southern Connecticut State College
New Haven, Connecticut

1976

January 22
East Carolina University
Greenville, North Carolina

January 27
Upper Arlington High School
Columbus, Ohio

January 29
University of Michigan
Detroit, Michigan

APPENDIX VII

1976 continued
May 1
Estherville High School
Estherville, Iowa

November 10
Fairleigh-Dickerson College
Rutherford, New Jersey

November 14
Longwood College
Farmville, Virginia

November 16
Ferrum College
Ferrum, Virginia

November 17
SUNY College
Oswego, New York

November 18
Oswego College
Oswego, New York

1977
January 31
University of Toledo
Toledo, Ohio

March 30
University of Colorado
Boulder, Colorado

1978
February 2
Niagara County Community College
Niagara Falls, New York

February 7
Bangor Community College
Bangor, Maine

Truth, Justice, & The American Way
The Life And Times Of Noel Neill
The Original Lois Lane

~ Acknowledgements ~

No book of any worth can be written without the help and assistance of others. This author endeavors to use this space to thank those who were instrumental in the development of this project.

To Noel Neill for countless months of interviews, and for openly sharing with me her thoughts and ideas, and her thousands of documents and photographs.

To Jack Larson for his wonderful introduction to this book, and for his friendship.

To LaVere and David Neill for collecting a fine series of scrapbooks of Noel's life over a period of almost fifty years. Every biographer should have the pleasure of such invaluable resources.

To Kathleen McCaslin for her never-ending support and encouragement.

To LeAnn McCaslin for her superior editing and astute editorial comments.

To Linda Steinour for her tireless work in typesetting this entire manuscript.

To the following for their friendship, advice, or encouragement: Joan Mazza; Phil Quinn, Linda Neill; Joe & Susan Magri; Jan Alan Henderson; Michael, Cindy, Ruth, & Fred Senseney; Tom Feldmann; Emily Oldak; Nick Peterson; Joe & Joan Warner; and to all the Fans of Superman.

To Manuel, June, Jackie, Connie, Marcia, Junette, Darryl, and my buddy Tim.

Finally, to Nicholas Lawrence Ward for being Nick.